The Next Stop

Inverness to Edinburgh
station by station

Simon Varwell

CONTENTS

ABOUT THE AUTHOR

Simon Varwell lives in Inverness, in the Highlands of Scotland, where he works in a really complicated job that takes ages to explain. In his spare time he loves travel, photography, exploring the great outdoors, and discovering the off-beat and unusual things that lurk amongst ordinary, everyday life.

This is his third book.

You can find out more about Simon's books and travels (including pictures from this book's journey), read some of his blog-based musings, and connect with him via social media at www.simonvarwell.co.uk.

BY THE SAME AUTHOR

Up The Creek Without a Mullet (2010, Sandstone Press)
The Return of the Mullet Hunter (2013)

ACKNOWLEDGEMENTS

Thanks first to my good friend Simon Bishop, who commented on a draft of this story and provided some very useful suggestions for improvement. If the book has any weaknesses, it's probably at the points where I didn't heed Simon's advice sufficiently.

Secondly, thanks to another good friend, Donald Noble, who designed the map of the route on page vii.

AUTHOR'S NOTE

I have changed the names and other biographical details of a few people who appear in this book.

Other than that, the story is exactly as it happened.

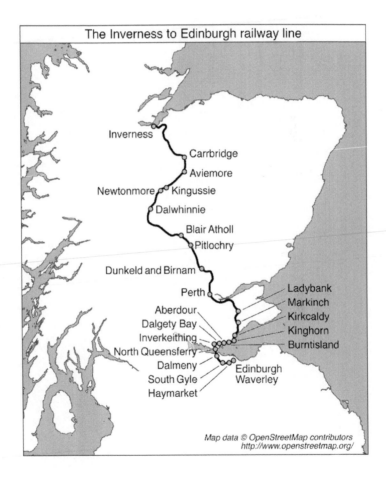

The Inverness to Edinburgh railway line

For Nicole

CHAPTER 1: INTRODUCTION

Sometimes we don't pay attention. We let things go past us in life without noticing them.

It's especially true of travelling. If we're on a journey for the first time through a beautiful area, our senses will be alert to the exciting new vistas. Perhaps doing it a second time, we'll notice something new. The novelty will wear off, though, on the third or fourth occasion. After that, when we've lost count of how many times we've done it, we'll stop looking. What's outside is no longer special, beautiful or noteworthy. It's routine, humdrum, ordinary.

This had become my problem.

Over the last few years I have regularly travelled by train between Inverness and Edinburgh for work, a journey of around three and a half hours. I live in Inverness, but my job for the last six years has required me to be in Edinburgh a few days a month.

I can't remember the first time I did that beautiful journey - probably many, many years ago, before I even moved to Inverness. So I no longer remember whether I was enthralled by the breath-taking views of the rugged Highland mountains, lush forests of Perthshire, or the Firth of Forth, where the line rushes through coastal towns and villages before crossing the

Forth Bridge, that spectacular icon of Victorian engineering.

I also have no idea how many times I've done the journey in either direction. It could be well over a hundred times.

The first departure of the day from Inverness is around a quarter to seven in the morning, a journey that feels like it starts in the middle of the night, suited white collar workers and yawning families gathering for the start of a long trip south; a journey that ends in Edinburgh at ten o'clock with my stomach craving lunch and my body craving sleep.

In the winter, that journey begins in the pitch dark, the sun rising spectacularly over the Cairngorm mountains forty or so minutes later. If doing a day trip, I return after the working day, the northbound journey enveloped in darkness outside and tiredness inside.

Even if I am away for a few days at a time, my journeys are rarely at more civilised times of the day. Outside the winter months, there's still little inclination to enjoy the scenery – there's too much work to catch up on, and working helps pass the time. Besides, I've seen the views through the window all too often. There's nothing new to see any more.

There are twenty-three stations on the line, including Inverness and Edinburgh themselves. However, trains rarely stop at more than half a dozen of them on any one service. The first half is the Highland Main Line between Inverness and Perth, with a few larger towns and villages regularly served, but also a number of small villages that see only a few stops per day.

From Perth to Edinburgh, the land is more heavily populated and the line overlaps for the final part with another route, the Fife Circle. This is a suburban loop service that starts and ends in Edinburgh and serves a large number of tightly packed towns and villages.

Over the years, though I knew the line well and could recite the stops in order from memory, I came to realise that I rarely paid attention to the scenery as it zipped past in a familiar blur. As the automatic voice on the train announcement system followed the "bing bong" and told us "the next stop is…" I rarely dwelled on what those next stops might be like.

I decided, therefore, that I ought to take time to explore the line. In part, I think, the idea was borne of a frustration that I was nearly always travelling the line for work – usually doing something productive, tapping away on my computer as I wrote reports or caught up with emails. Sometimes, whether through exhaustion of either mind or laptop battery (or both), I would read a book, listen to music through my earphones or just gaze vacantly out of the window.

On the few occasions when I'd travel the line for personal reasons, and be free from the work laptop to appreciate the journey, still I'd just read, listen to music, snooze or sit back and relax, knowing I didn't have to pay attention to anything or worry about work.

But I soon concluded that the places the line ran through were as unfamiliar to me as some of the most evocative destinations abroad that I had long wanted to visit. I began to play around with the idea of travelling the line to find out more about it and to see what I was missing. The unknown, after all, can often be right under our noses.

A number of options arose in my mind. One was to walk it, allowing me to explore the often rugged and barren landscape and amble at leisure through the towns and villages the line served. I could explore the more curious sights that lay between the stations – stretches of forest or river like the spectacular Killiecrankie pass, high up on a steep cliff, glimpsed only briefly every time the train rushed past. I could peer inside abandoned buildings such as the remains of closed stations. I could step back from the line and see its most impressive parts, such as the dramatic viaducts I had so often passed over. It would be an up-close and intimate exploration of the line at a radically different pace, though at over a hundred and fifty miles it would require significant levels of fitness, some serious logistical planning and a lot of time off.

Another possibility was to do the same but by car, earning

me significant freedom to go where I wanted, both at and between the stations. However, I wasn't a huge fan of driving, and it would seem odd, perhaps even cheating, to do a journey about a railway line by means of a car.

I should do the trip by rail, I then decided, stopping at every single station. While it would have been rewarding to see the bits in between the stations, I found I was most intrigued by the towns and villages I never stopped at, the scheduled stops I just zipped through without dwelling on, except for half-hearing the tannoy announcements or glimpsing the blurred spires of their churches or the nameless faces waiting on the platforms.

I knew that trains ran south from Inverness at least every two hours, and a minimum of two hours was probably a good length of time to get a flavour of each town or village before catching the next train. On that basis I could complete the journey in about a week.

I was somewhat aided in the decision to go by train thanks to a slow but steady accumulation of compensation vouchers from rail companies. One consequence of regular train travel is being the victim of occasional delays – for instance through bad weather or a mechanical fault. Many extended days, frustrating waits at stations, and rail replacement buses had meant that in the past year or so I'd gained vouchers that added up to a substantial value. That meant lots of train journeys to take, but so little free time in which to take them.

So I settled on a week, in the spring of 2012. I reasoned the weather would be not too hot or cold, and it would be a nice balance between the height of the summer tourist rush and the quiet of winter when not much, especially in smaller places, would be open.

The plan was simple. What could be a better way of looking at the stops along a railway line than by getting off and exploring each one? I looked forward to tallying up my fleeting glimpses from a train with a close up view on foot, and finding out what the places were like, what made them tick and what might make a visitor return.

Other than the logistics of timetabling and organising accommodation along the way, I intentionally did very little background research into the places I would be visiting. For a start, to research over twenty different locations would have been time-consuming. But more than that, I wanted to allow the destinations to speak for themselves. The less I knew about them, the better, because my lack of expectation or prior understanding would allow each stop to present itself in its own way. I would be able to look at each place with a fresh, objective eye: as a visitor, tourist, stranger. A stranger in my own country, keen to discover the unknown adventures that lay on my doorstep.

So I worked out a timetable, booked a week off work, packed a small bag, and on a bright Monday morning in April I left the house and walked down to Inverness railway station.

CHAPTER 2: CARRBRIDGE

It was Monday, 8.43am, and I was on the train and ready to leave Inverness. At last I was beginning to feel just a little excited, which I hadn't at all when my wife Nicole had asked me while we ate breakfast. I wondered whether I ought to have been a bit more alive to the adventure ahead, but it felt just like any old Monday morning with a train south to catch.

This one, though, was the start of an unusual journey, and when I boarded and saw "Carrbridge" on the scrolling list of destinations on the electronic screen, I began to look forward to the many places that lay ahead.

I found a seat, sat back and relaxed, ready and eager to savour this inaugural journey. Inverness looked no different out of the train window, though I suspected the sense of adventure and real "new" would come at Carrbridge. It was quite appropriate that the first stop should be one I didn't know at all.

"It's quiet, isn't it? I thought it would be mobbed."

I realised an old woman with a stick across the aisle was talking to me. She was heading to Glasgow, she told me. She was glad she was not on an Edinburgh train, she said, or else she'd have required a change at Perth.

"You have to lug all your bags across Perth station and it's hard if you've not booked assistance."

"Right," I said, my introspection interrupted. The fact that I was, for once, not sitting with music in my ears and my head in a laptop and was a little more alert to my surroundings must have made me seem ripe for conversation. Not that I minded, of course. It was a novelty to be talking to a fellow passenger for once.

The weather was nice, she declared, a dry day and not too cold. I spotted an advertising billboard next to the railway line with tantalising images of the sunshine of Tunisia.

"Though I am just up for the weekend from Stirling."

"Right," I said again, unsure of what I could bring to the conversation.

A pause. The train began to move.

"My name's Diane."

Apparently we were at the name-swapping stage.

I introduced myself, and this opened the floodgates to Diane's life story. She had lived in Inverness some years before retiring, and had worked in retail. She'd studied business at college in Aberdeen as a young woman, and then worked there in a department store as a management trainee. She moved around various departments, including children's ("the noise of the toys just never stopped") and corsetry ("the men were the funniest customers"). She said it taught her a lot about inequality ("it was fourteen pounds per week for women, twenty-one for men – doing the same job!"), she was treated badly, and the managers were very poor.

Then she and her fiancé had talked about going for a break to the Iona Community, a Christian organisation based in the historic abbey on the island of Iona. The break somehow turned into a career change when the opportunity of work as an assistant chef had somehow arisen. But she'd misinterpreted the idea of "assistant chef", thinking it was more of a kitchen hand. She arrived on the chef's day off, and needed to cook single-handedly for seventy people straight away.

"I couldn't swim back – people had tried and died," she said earnestly, as if this was a form of escape she had seriously contemplated. The chef cancelled her day off and taught her to cook in a day. One dish she learned was boiled chicken, cooked in a huge urn.

"I hope they didn't mix it up with the tea urn," I quipped.

"Well, no it was much bigger," she said, completely missing my joke, "but yes that's a good point."

Our conversation paused as the refreshments trolley came by. Diane got some soup and tea from the man attending it, and used his name, which she read from his badge. She had been regularly using my name as she spoke to me too. Perhaps she'd been a schoolteacher in a past life.

The train was a bit bumpy and we were going fast at this stage not far south of Inverness, having hit the top of the hill behind Culloden that represents the first challenge for southbound trains.

"On a ship, you need sea legs," said the trolley attendant, standing steadily as he pumped tea from the flask. "Here you need train legs."

Diane talked all the way to Carrbridge. It was odd to speak to someone – or more accurately be spoken at – for the whole of the journey, and I got only fleeting glimpses of Inverness as we departed and of the landscape along the way. Part of me had wanted the time to myself to take in the scenery and enjoy the start of my epic trip. Yet Diane, for all her gentle eccentricity, was perfectly pleasant and friendly, and it was a reminder to me to be open to all the unknown and unexpected interactions that might lie ahead in the coming week.

Had I the opportunity to just gaze out of the window, though, there would have been much to take in during that first half hour to Carrbridge. For instance, we passed abandoned stations, now overgrown and easily missed. They included Daviot, Moy and Tomatin, and the goods yard and platforms at Culloden Moor. They were all closed in the infamous Beeching Axe of the 1960s, when around a third of Britain's railway network was scrapped in one of the century's stupidest government decisions. Carrbridge was the sole survivor between Inverness and Aviemore.

These stations had served villages that still exist and flourish. Added to them, new suburban sprawl alongside the line closer to Inverness, such as at Culloden or the retail park and new university campus, suggested that the line surely had so much potential for the future – both through new stations and renewed life in those casualties of Beeching.

When first completed in the mid-nineteenth century, the line involved travelling north to Inverness via Forres, a town some distance to the east. The line branched off at Aviemore towards Grantown on Spey to avoid some steep hills and a couple of rivers, and then looped back westwards at Forres towards Inverness. However these technical challenges were later overcome when a "short cut" between Aviemore and Inverness was built. It opened in 1898 and included the Tomatin and Clava viaducts, magnificent pieces of Victorian engineering that were true icons of the local area. The Clava viaduct was a particularly impressive sight from ground level. At thirty-nine metres high and over five hundred metres long, the twenty-nine arches of solid sandstone made for the longest stone railway viaduct in the country.

Meanwhile, the line from Aviemore to Grantown on Spey and Forres lost its reason for being, and Beeching's axe swung.

At quarter past nine on the morning of that first day, I was the only passenger getting off. The station was quiet, apart from a man in a Scotrail hi-vis vest wandering around, obviously undertaking an inspection. We exchanged hellos as he passed me. He went to an intercom on the platform and pressed a button. He introduced himself as a "quality auditor. Could you do a sound check please?" A generic announcement came over the tannoy and the man ticked something on his clipboard.

I sat at the station for a few moments to collect my thoughts and sort my bag out. I was carrying only one small rucksack, which contained a few clothes and toiletries, plus other bits and bobs like my notebook and camera. I was glad to be able to travel light given I'd be taking the bag everywhere with me.

I left the deathly quiet station, and walked down what appeared to be the main road towards the village centre. However, I soon saw a sign for an alternative riverside walk to the village so I decided to take that instead.

It was a bright, sunny spring day, free from breeze but a little cool. I had three hours in Carrbridge. I had no idea what to expect, but hoped I wouldn't be too bored.

Pretty wood carvings of animals such as owls and squirrels dotted the roadside. One, standing next to a house, appeared to be either a squirrel or wildcat, with a very sinister-looking human face like a hideous cathedral gargoyle. It was standing on its front legs, its face at the base and its long, bushy tail pointing high upwards above its body. The carvings were all very beautiful and incredibly detailed.

I reached the river. Green fields stretched along the far bank, a few horses standing idly here and there, and large houses lay beyond. The houses I could see, and those I saw later elsewhere in the village, were a mix of big Victorian mansions, modest old cottages, some 1970s bungalows, and modern Scandinavian-style wooden eco-houses with steep roofs and large windows.

I crossed the river via a modest wooden footbridge, where a sign instructed me "no fishing", and I followed the path alongside the fields. A jogger passed by me in the other direction, her footsteps pounding the bridge as she went over it, and once she was gone there was silence once more.

Further down the track I passed a dilapidated stone shed, which backed on to some sort of warehouse or workshop, and outside sat the rusting remains of a small bus or delivery vehicle that looked like it was from the 1950s at the latest.

I arrived in the centre of the village, the focus of which was the old packhorse bridge spanning the river Dulnain. Though I had never visited Carrbridge and knew little about the village, I had heard of the bridge and had seen one or two photographs of it online.

Built in 1717, it was a modest and thin structure, almost

defying gravity as it rose and dropped over the river with a curious steepness. This was due to a massive spate in 1829 that washed much of it away leaving only this spindly, fragile frame. It now stood fenced off, inaccessible and looking somewhat forlorn.

The bridge made for an odd focal point for the centre of the village, with roads on the riverbanks either side and the more modern road bridge looming over it from just a few metres away. Its setting, low against its surroundings, made it seem smaller than it was, and I only really appreciated its scale when I crossed the road bridge and descended some steps on the other side of the river to stand on a modest platform. Shaded by the high banks and the road bridge, the spot rendered great views of the old bridge. There was a certain angle for photographing it that cut out the houses, roads and indeed anything modern around it – framing just the bridge, the river flowing under it, and thick trees in the background.

A couple of other camera-wielding tourists were around (yes, I thought I counted as one on my trip) but I soon had the spot to myself. I sat down and fished some sandwiches out of my bag. I ate, drank some water and enjoyed the view for a while before continuing my exploration.

The centre of Carrbridge wasn't much to speak of, though it was not unattractive. Near the packhorse bridge lay a junction. This was where the road through the village met another that ran eastwards from the A9 towards Speyside and Deeside. At the junction, the unimaginatively named Carrbridge Hotel stood, a grand old inn that had apparently been a stopping point for a couple of centuries.

I headed away from the junction and along the main street through the village, past a couple of shops. It was surprisingly busy for a Monday. Two men passed, pushing prams. A muddy field was on my right, inhabited by a pig that was sniffing out a couple of tourists that had stopped to say hello to it.

Further on, I passed the parish church, a small but pretty building set back a little from the road. Its sign bore multilingual greetings, though the German "Willkommen" had been either faded or misspelt to read "Willkommer", which I hoped didn't mean anything too rude in German.

Not far before it looked like I would run out of village to explore I found the entrance sign for the Landmark activity centre. I was glad to have found it, because it was the only feature of Carrbridge other than the packhorse bridge I could recall having heard of, and I had had no idea how far out of the village it was.

A giant family-friendly outdoor adventure playground, Landmark boasted, among other things, a large wooden tower that, from pictures I'd seen, rendered great views of the hills and forests around. As a lone male I feared I would feel slightly self-conscious among the target market of young families and children, and in any case I didn't feel the entry fee would be justified in the short time that I had, so I continued past.

Running along the side of the Landmark complex, instead, was a path heading into the trees. "Fàilte" a sign said, welcoming me to "Ellan Wood". A simple map on the sign suggested that there was quite a spider's web of paths to explore, so I headed away from the road and bright sunshine into the relative peace and shade. The different paths connected together and made for a walk of an hour or so in total. At one point it took me right round the back of Landmark and just the other side of a fence from its famous big tower. Even standing almost directly underneath it, it didn't actually appear that tall, though composed entirely of wood the tower looked like it wasn't a pleasant ascent for anyone who (like me) didn't have a good head for heights.

I passed a few more carved owls, standing with lifelike alertness, and the occasional wooden bench, one with two enormous, pointed beams of wood at the back. I sat in it briefly and felt like one of the bad guys from a Tolkien story. The sunlight scattered through the tall trees to throw a patchwork of light and long shadows upon the soft undergrowth. I seemed to have the paths to myself.

Further round, I came across the train line. The path ran

for a short section right alongside the single-track railway, and I paused for a moment at this spot, imagining a train shooting past, an alternative me glimpsed at a carriage window, head down, not noticing. I could now know that this wasn't just any random bit of forest but one particular place I had stood in. All was silent. In the background stood a mountain capped with a dusting of snow. I checked the timetable in my pocket but found no imminent trains to wait for, so I pressed on.

I soon found myself at Carrbridge's graveyard. I find graveyards fascinating because they are great windows into a community. They indicate something of the history of a place, as – especially in older headstones – you see mention of often now obsolete occupations; and the names of places and families help to bring the place, ironically, to life. Many names, though long gone, are still alive in the thoughts and memories of others. In this graveyard I saw fresh flowers on one or two gravestones of people who had been dead for many decades: fading names, perhaps even fading memories, but a love as vivid as ever. I noted a few headstones of tragically young children, one relatively recent one with some bright, colourful flowers and a small toy car, its red paint paled by the elements.

Intriguingly, I found two or three headstones marking the graves of foresters from Newfoundland. One of them, according to the inscription, had been accidentally shot. While it would seem natural that workers from that great land of forests should find work in Scotland from time to time, it intrigued me that the foresters' deaths all seemed to be during the Second World War. Later research led me to discover that men from the Canadian Forestry Corps, part of the Canadian Army, had been stationed near Carrbridge. Presumably with the labour shortage caused by the conflict, overseas manpower was a vital part of Britain's war effort. Interestingly, Newfoundland was still a separate dominion at the time, and only became a part of Canada in 1949. How sadly ironic that a number of young men would, perhaps thinking their posting a safe one compared to the horrors of the European combat, meet their end through what could well have been avoidable industrial accidents.

On a small hill in the middle of the cemetery sat a bench, with a plaque dedicating it to a couple "in a place they loved". Really? Cemeteries are interesting places, but I couldn't imagine going as far as to say I loved them, not least given the range of sad stories they contain.

Not far away from the cemetery was the war memorial. It was curiously tucked away out of obvious sight at the top of a thickly forested hill, with little in the way of a sense of place and not much much space to assemble a congregation. There was birdsong in the air and a bright morning sun, and only the shade of the trees and a slight breeze to counter its warmth.

It almost felt like re-emerging into reality as I came down the hill and hit the main street again. There was a pleasant café across the road, where I imbibed a hot chocolate and some cake. I sat writing notes for about half an hour and reflected on my morning's explorations.

The café was a bustling wee place, with a number of other customers coming and going while I was there. Across the room from me there was a young Chinese couple, perhaps in their twenties, talking in halting English to an older couple who were, I guessed by their accents, from the south of England. They were having a polite conversation about something to do with Chinese history. I wondered in vain precisely what the relationship between the two couples might have been.

Next to me was a family with two young children having lunch after, it seemed, being out for a walk.

Later, what I think was a German couple came in, though they didn't stay for long and left before me, using the café just as an excuse for a toilet stop. When the waitress came to take their orders, she found herself in what struck me – and perhaps her – as an odd conversation in which she had to explain what a double espresso was.

As much as my people-watching was modest entertainment, the café was starting to busy up for lunch, so I decided to leave. I had an hour left until my onward train and didn't really know what else to do. I checked my mobile phone, but found I had no signal whatsoever. For now, I had plenty battery remaining, but knew I would have to conserve it, having uncharacteristically left my charger at home.

Back across the road from the café was a gallery. My spectacular lack of interest in art was outweighed by the fact I had nothing else to do and plenty time to kill, and so I went in for a browse.

I was greeted immediately by an inquisitive and friendly Yorkshire terrier, evidently owned by the middle-aged woman behind the counter. I said hello as I perused the range of sculptures, pictures and pottery.

"We do it all ourselves," she said when I asked about the place. "Me, my husband" – she nodded through the door into the back part of the gallery, where a man was seated at a desk, painting – "and our daughter. We do it all here. Apart from the wood carving, though, that's done elsewhere."

I didn't think at the time to ask whether they were responsible for all the carved owls and squirrels I'd seen around the village. If so, they had a veritable stranglehold on Carrbridge's visual arts scene.

It was all very lovely, but I really didn't have the inclination, money or space in my small bag for any works of art. After a thorough wander round and a few friendly pats of the dog's head, I said thanks to the woman and left.

Despite having plenty time until my train I found myself drifting back to the railway station, simply because it would be a place where I could comfortably hang out, enjoy a sit down and do nothing.

The station was empty, the quality auditor from earlier presumably long gone. I wandered around the outside of the station buildings, now abandoned but which back in its heyday would have been staffed and a lot busier. Peering through some windows, I could see a row of empty coat hangers and a large wooden cupboard as only the features in what I guessed would have been the old station office before it was unstaffed. A fading Top Gear car sticker was in one window, featuring a BBC logo from the mid-1990s.

Alongside the station was a builders' yard, containing piles of wood, old machinery, a caravan and a shed. Curiously, an old red phone box stood proudly in the middle of the yard, surveying the silence. There was little indication as to whether the place ever saw life.

Next to it was a siding, a short and heavily overgrown stretch of line that I imagined might have been used in the past for loading and unloading from the builders' yard or whatever operation was there before it. I stepped down off the platform into the undergrowth and walked between the rusting tracks. The undergrowth was not far off completely hiding any evidence of the line. With the platform on one side, a fence on the other, and tall trees towering all around, this little siding seemed forgotten, a ghost of industry and movement past.

I climbed the steps onto the bridge over the main line, and walked to the middle, directly over the two tracks. Much of the route south to Perth was single track but here, as at other stations down the line, there was a second one allowing two trains to pass. I could see for some distance, forested hills surrounding the village. It was a beautiful spot, though with the station empty of other passengers and the haunting dereliction of the overgrown siding and builders' yard, there was a real sense of abandonment in the stillness.

In time, my train arrived. It had taken me nearly half an hour at the start of the morning to reach Carrbridge, in what would be one of the longest legs of the whole journey. The next leg would only be eight minutes, taking me to Aviemore.

CHAPTER 3: AVIEMORE

I sat as close to the door as I could for this short journey. Two women in the seats behind me, who had obviously been on from Inverness, were chatting away. Rather delightfully, one of them was talking about how it was hard to really appreciate the scenery en route. She said she often went up and down the line, but everything had become too familiar.

Well, indeed. That reassured me that I was doing the right thing in trying to explore the line in such detail.

In my few minutes on board, the topic of the women's conversation shifted to one of the two's recent travels in Australia and then something about the Gaelic primary school in Inverness. It was quite a rally of conversation topics. I hoped they wouldn't run out of chat before their destination and have to face prolonged, awkward silences. Part of me was tempted to turn round and suggest that they pace themselves a little better.

I arrived in Aviemore to find rain. I didn't dwell too long in the railway station itself, though it was certainly worth lingering in. Home also to the Strathspey Steam Railway, the building was a beautiful and well-kept old structure with red painted trims and an intricate canopy, and had an evocative sense of the past about it. But I knew I would have plenty time to linger later on, if Carrbridge was anything to go by, as I had four and a half hours to kill here.

I didn't try to take in much of Aviemore when I first headed on to the main street. Partly it was because I knew the town quite well – it was a major tourist resort, a key stop-off for the Cairngorms, and I had passed through and stopped often. Apart from Inverness and Edinburgh, Aviemore was probably the town I knew best on the line. Partly, also, it was because the town's centre is not much to look at. While the railways provided its first major growth, tourism in the 1960s – particularly skiing – provided another. Drab and uninspiring architecture inevitably accompanied this, and the main street was, with a few proud Victorian exceptions, aesthetically uninteresting, with a host of outdoor stores, tourist shops and restaurants housed within bland modern shopping complexes that looked like they'd been transported from suburban North America.

But my main reason not to linger was that I had a mission. Having left my phone charger behind when leaving home that morning, I wanted to find a replacement. My iPhone, as ever, was going to be a key tool on my journey. I would need it to check things on the map, search for places on the internet if I needed, and of course keep in touch with Nicole back home. Even switching it off when I wasn't using it wouldn't stop the battery completely draining, so I knew I had to have a good search around town for somewhere that sold chargers. Of course, if I ended up seeing Aviemore along the way, then great.

I walked up and down the main street in the town centre, but the only two likely options, a computer shop and an electrical store, were both closed that day, it being the Easter Monday bank holiday. The tourist information centre was open and busy, however, and once I'd fought my way through the crowds a man at the desk had no further ideas as to where else would sell it.

My walk reminded me of what a nondescript place

Aviemore was. It wasn't particularly ugly, in fact far from it. It was clean, bright and backdropped by rich greens and browns from the forests and hillsides, including the Cairngorm mountains over to the east. The town was clearly all about the outdoors, with the streets of full of people kitted up for cycling or hiking. I overheard a range of accents, too, Aviemore drawing people from far and wide.

But that sprawl of dull, modern shopping arcades and buildings was merely an attempt to fling up stuff to meet the demand of the tourist trade. The MacDonald Resort, a huge hotel and leisure chain complex, towered over the west side of the main street. I'd heard various stories over the years about how locals were not too impressed with the resort, tending as it supposedly did to employ foreign labour rather than local workers.

One place of interest was the Waterstone's bookshop, which I briefly popped into for a look around. It was a very small store and had a strong focus, naturally, on the outdoors and tourism. I noted with only very mild disappointment that my first book from two years previously wasn't on the shelf.

I also popped into the small WH Smiths newsagents on the off-chance they might have an iPhone charger. They didn't, but they did suggest I try Tesco. I figured I'd do that later. No point blowing all the fun in the first hour of my time in Aviemore.

On a whim, and deciding I wanted to get away from this soulless gallery of 1960s architecture, I followed a footpath at the south end of the town centre near the WH Smith and found myself by the river. It was instantly quieter, though with numerous groups of people on foot or bike passing by. The river itself was calm and beautifully clear. The light rain I'd arrived to had stopped, and the sky had turned a bright blue, the sun providing some modest springtime warmth.

I walked over a small bridge and along the path only to find myself back at a busy road, one that led to the pretty shores of Loch Morlich and onwards into the Cairngorms. It was too far to venture in the few hours I had, and I didn't want to drift too far from town. I told myself that the trip was about the actual towns and villages that were home to the railway stations, and not really the wider countryside around or in between. Plus, I'd passed a pub on my way out and I figured it was probably time for a drink. The afternoon was getting on and, after all, I was on holiday.

The Old Bridge Inn seemed a popular place, and I was sure I'd heard the name before. Inside was surprisingly dark and busy for the time of day, with most of the loud chatter coming from one drunk guy at the bar. A barmaid was talking to him and seemed glad to be able to break away from his ramblings to serve me. It looked like the sort of pub that would do good live music, and be a real hub at nights. The food smelled good too.

It was tempting to stay inside and see what craic was going on. However I had taken an instant dislike to the noisy drunk, and given that it was a warm and bright afternoon I decided to sit in the sunshine at one of the tables on the grass just across the road.

It was quiet outside, with three guys in cycling gear the only other outdoor customers. They sat a couple of tables away, their bicycles nearby on the ground. I noticed with intrigue that they were all drinking pints. I knew the rules about drink driving, but had to admit that my understanding of the laws on drink cycling was a mite fuzzier.

I took a sip of my pint. I was only on shandy. There was an impressive range of real ales on tap inside, and not far from Aviemore was the Cairngorm Brewery, one of the Highlands' many small independent breweries, of which I was quite a fan. However, I figured I should pace myself. I had a whole evening to spend in Kingussie later on in the day, and finding a pub somewhere in a quiet Highland town on a bank holiday evening might transpire to be my best and indeed only option for something to do. And anyway, it was a warm spring afternoon, and the crisp, refreshing shandy did quite the trick. I could hear birdsong. A few people were walking along the river down to my right. The occasional car passed by.

I jotted some notes in my book and wondered what I was going to do for the next three hours. A bit more of a walk, perhaps, if I could find a nice track to explore. Tesco, to check for phone chargers. And of course the steam railway, which I could leave to last as it was right next to the main railway line where I would catch my next train south.

I heard a train close by. I looked up to my left, behind the pub, and there was a jet of blue Scotrail livery whooshing by from the south towards Aviemore station. I realised then that the large building beside the pub was a bunkhouse I would regularly see from the train. I was glad that I was being true to the journey by seeing something from a different angle from how I usually saw it. Again I imagined myself aboard, shooting past in a blur, indistinguishable even as the train slowed down for its stop.

It looked from the passing trade that the pub was getting a little busier, but it remained just the three cyclists and me outside. As it was cooling slightly I had a choice to make. I decided against a second pint, tempting though that was, and figured I should press onwards with my exploring.

I ambled down the modest incline to the river, and found a path alongside. It turned into a fairly decent loop from the pub, along the riverside and back into town through some trees and a field. Across the river, the Cairngorm mountains lay, snow on the higher ground and encroached by low clouds. The Cairngorm range was one of the best regions in Scotland for outdoor activities from hillwalking to skiing to mountain biking. Aviemore and a few smaller surrounding villages were economically dependent on tourism, though while I had done quite a bit of walking in the wider area over the years this was probably the most I had explored the town itself.

At one point towards the end of my walk it wasn't clear how to get across a field and back towards town, but I asked a couple of men that were passing by in the opposite direction, one curiously carrying a golf club despite being nowhere near a golf course as far as I could see. They pointed me in the right direction and I arrived back at the railway station just in time, happily, to see a steam train pull in.

The Strathspey Railway was originally part of the line that went all the way to Forres, and of course onwards from there to Inverness. Following its closure by Beeching, a band of volunteers got together in the 1970s to reopen part of it as a steam railway. The line stretched only a couple of stops north, a slow forty-five minute journey that I had never done but kept telling myself I should do one day.

There were plans, though, to extend the line a little further along its former route to Grantown on Spey. The company was currently attempting to raise the money to undertake the work; a task, of course, that should never have been necessary. The removal of the line was one of countless closures that were a devastating blow to rural Britain, and many towns and villages that lost their rail link have never been quite the same again.

The steam train let out a large whistle as it chugged into the station, the glistening black engine pumping smoke into the air as it puffed to a halt. The thick smell filled the air, temporarily evoking a bygone age of travel before the slightly less romantic smell of diesel took over the railways. I was one of more than a handful of folk wielding cameras to catch it as it came in, and the platform soon filled with passengers as they alighted. The train was, appropriately enough, a beautiful old steam train immaculately and no doubt lovingly restored, and its black livery glinted in the sunlight. The crew, all apparently volunteers, were kitted out in peaked caps and old-fashioned railway uniforms or overalls.

Next to the platform, a sign pointed me into the old station shop. It was a silent and pokey little place with an awkward small town library feel to it. I felt like I was being watched by the woman behind the desk. The shop had an obvious focus on trains, with an odd collection of retro and faux-retro railway signs and postcards, jigsaws and model railway pieces, plus more unexpected tat such as plastic dinosaurs and children's books. It was an unappealing hotchpotch.

After that, with still over an hour and a half until my train, I sat for a few minutes on the platform to take the weight off my feet after all the walking I'd done. I then headed back up the main street to Tesco, where I searched – to no avail, alas – for a phone charger. Hungry, I realised it was around five o'clock in the afternoon so I headed across the road to a chippy and ordered some food. It was a busy place I'd been to a number of times on passing through the town. I ordered my usual king rib supper and onion rings, the same as what you'd get in any chippy but good, simple sustenance. Much as chippies are dependable places, there's probably not much art to the food, but I was hungry after an afternoon's exploring, and art was not what I was seeking.

I sat at one of the outside tables to eat, watching the BBC News channel on the TV through the window, the amusingly inaccurate subtitles providing the only real alternative to watching an endless procession of Gore-Tex walking up and down the street.

Heading the short distance along the bland street back to the station, I realised that nearly all the shops that I had seen in Aviemore were chains – not least the multitude of shops selling outdoor gear. I saw very few independent places beyond the occasional café. Earlier, I had noticed an empty butcher's shop, not far from Tesco. A sign in its window said they were now closed and thanked people for thirteen years' custom.

Just up the line from the platform lay evidence that it was a much bigger station in the past. When the line to Forres was still in existence this junction must have been a busy place, as there was a large yard and a few buildings long since abandoned and gated off. Some of the siding appeared to be still in use by the steam railway, but the buildings themselves looked forlorn and neglected. Paint was peeling on the doors. Weeds were growing here and there. A sign on an old footbridge over the line read "KEEP OFF". It was metres – yet decades – from the bustle of the main station.

Returning to the station, I sat down on a bench on the platform where in thirty minutes my train would arrive. The sun was hiding behind clouds and it was getting chilly. I could have been somewhere warm, like a café or pub. I was getting used to the idea of being on a wee adventure with no responsibilities to worry about, and so the prospect of another pint somewhere was tempting. But I told myself I'd had one earlier and might need to depend on a couple for something to do later that night.

Plus, I'd seen pretty much all Aviemore had to offer in the allotted time without breaking the point of the trip and heading into the hills. I'd done what I had set out to do – to find out whether Aviemore was interesting in itself and was worth a revisit. While a great base for the outdoors and a fine locus for eats and drinks at the end of an active day, the town itself was nothing better than functional, and frankly more than a little dull.

I hoped my next two stops were not as uninspiring. I had an evening and morning in Kingussie followed by an afternoon in Newtonmore, and I doubted that either would be big enough to be worth even spending time looking for a phone charger in.

CHAPTER 4: KINGUSSIE

The journey to Kingussie was just a few uneventful minutes down the line. It was a place I don't remember ever having visited, at least certainly not by train, and my first impressions were good.

The majority of Kingussie was on the west side of the railway line, with the only real landmark on the other side being the rather ugly and modern secondary school. The centre of Kingussie, however, was much more pleasant, and had its roots in a planned town, conceived and built around the beginning of the nineteenth century. Boasting a grand, if slightly austere Victorian style, its heart was a small and easy to navigate grid system of grey stone buildings, centring on a large park that led from the station to the main road. I would be spending the night in the town, so I headed down the road towards where I was staying, a small bunkhouse connected to a pub that was the cheapest place in town I could find.

The main street was quiet. It was after six o'clock and shops were mostly closed, but to my surprise a computer and video rental store was still open. I went in, wondering if it was a good place to try for a phone charger. The friendly man behind the counter, thankfully, sold just what I needed. We chatted briefly. He spoke with a strong Dutch accent.

"Four and a half yearsh here, and it'sh shtill brilliant."

That was reassuring. I only needed it to be brilliant until lunchtime the following day.

The pub, just a few doors further down the main street, was quite busy. It had an air of unpretentious amiability about it.

A lassie behind the bar told me that the entrance to the bunkhouse was round the back, and pointed me back outside where I found a passageway along the side of the pub. I met her at the back door and she showed me through another door across the small courtyard and up some clanging metal steps to my room. It was a small and cramped space; drab, but clean and functional. The lack of luxury mattered not; I was only going to be here a night.

There were two bunk beds and a single bed, though the young woman said I would have the room to myself that night. She pointed out the kitchen on the ground floor, which I was welcome to use, then showed me where the bathroom was.

"The men's showers are a bit manky, but there's no women in tonight so you can just use the women's showers."

After dumping my bag and deciding my tiny room wasn't worth hanging around in longer than necessary, I headed out to see the sights.

On second impression, Kingussie didn't feel as engaging as on the first.

Admittedly it was a weekday evening in April and the sky just turning dark, but I was surprised at how little life there was. There were few people and little traffic on the streets, and no lively pub except the one I was staying at, just a couple of rather empty-looking hotel bars elsewhere along the main road. The town seemed quite content in its own little world, a bit prim and proper, with neat houses lining the grey, linear streets.

I passed a church a little further down the main road, set back on a small hill and surrounded by gravestones. It was a modest and unremarkable building, a typical old parish church that bore testament to the Calvinistic tastes and no doubt empty pockets of the past century or two in the Highlands. I took a wander around the small graveyard, each headstone casting a long shadow in the low, setting sun. Some headstones were more ornate than others, and represented the usual silent army of the deceased, some dating back over a hundred years.

One headstone from the late nineteenth century commemorated a man "who was parish teacher for 16 months". He had died, it seemed, at the tragically young age of twenty-five, with no cause of death mentioned. It had cut short what perhaps would have been a long and happy career in the village, though the inscription was rounded off with the striking words "Deeply regretted".

It seemed an odd choice of phrase, "regret" being the sort of cautious word used by politicians who admit they did something wrong but don't want to actually say "sorry". "Deeply regretted" might perhaps have been a polite code on the part of the villagers – they regretted, maybe, having to bury their teacher and recruit another one, but actually everyone silently detested him and they couldn't bring themselves to lie and say "sadly missed". Of course, the fact that there was no cause of death suggested an even darker secret – had the teacher done something to warrant his murder? Sixteen months would be more than long enough to put several noses out of joint in a small place like Kingussie…

I peeled myself away from my Wicker Man-style conspiracies and pressed on. Leaving the road I approached what seemed to be a very overgrown builder's yard, where a rickety shed stood. A pile of wood sat nearby, with a sign warning me that:

> "Any person removing goods from these premises without authority will be prosecuted."

– presumably not, I thought, if they turned up on a quiet evening when nobody was watching.

Nearby was an old thatched cottage, a muddy path leading

up to it. This, I knew from having passed it on the train so many times, was formerly part of the Highland Folk Museum. Now entirely based at Newtonmore, and something I had in mind for a visit when I got there the following afternoon, this small "offshoot" at Kingussie had recently been closed. The thatched cottages, if indeed they were original, stood abandoned for a second time.

I heard the rush of a huge train and looked over to where the railway line ran. Checking the time on my watch, I saw it was around seven o'clock and I realised that it would be the East Coast train from London that would arrive in Inverness around an hour later. There was one daytime service in each direction that connected Inverness to the UK's capital, an eight-hour journey I've done only once or twice. More often, though, I've taken the East Coast just between Inverness and Edinburgh. I took a photo of the long, rigid snake of carriages as it shot past.

I continued my amble through the village. Being the main settlement for some distance, not least a long way southwards, Kingussie was a historically important centre with a number of ornate civic buildings, modest in one sense but grand by Kingussie's standards. I also passed the bowling club, founded in 1877.

Back up towards the other end of the village, I saw a sign pointing me westwards and up the hills towards some forest walks. "Discover the Gynack – the golden burn at the heart of Kingussie" read an interpretation board. It was still just about light enough for a walk, so I followed the signs along a circular path up around the town that was punctuated by a series of panels about the town's mill heritage. They explained that the town, previously just a scattering of small agricultural settlements, was developed as a centre for wool and linen mills, and the burn was dammed in places to supply the many mills. None now remained, and the one mill structure still standing had become a restaurant and hotel. I also learned that with the nineteenth century arrival of the railway, Kingussie became an important tourist destination, and the famous writer Robert Louis Stevenson was among its visitors.

It was an attractive walk aside from all the historical information, and the mountains and thick forests to the west of the village towards which I was headed would be great vantage points for views across Kingussie and the open countryside in the other direction.

Soon the loop brought me back into the village, which was no bad thing as it was getting quite dark. I arrived at a modest tower by a road, standing alone and overlooking Kingussie. Built in 1925, according to the inscription, it was a sharp and angular construction with clock faces and a bell that struck each hour, audible across the village in the silent night air.

It wasn't long before I found myself back at the pub I was staying in. I ordered a beer and found a quiet seat in the corner where I sat and read. The pub was an L-shaped tale of two halves, and I was right in the middle. The part to my right was the restaurant where a few folk were eating, in front of me was the bar, and on my left was a pool table and a rowdy, if harmless, group of folk who were clearly regulars and having a good few drinks and games of pool. Two women, including the one who had shown me my room earlier, were serving table and running the bar, and I could see a couple of men in the kitchen at the back of the restaurant. Surveying the clientele, I made a guess that I was the only non-local in that evening.

I had a couple of drinks, reading happily and quietly, and then went to my room. The bed was comfy despite being quite small. It had been a fairly full first day, after all, taking in Carrbridge, Aviemore and now Kingussie. All the fresh air and walking, not to mention the couple of pints, helped me sleep soundly.

I woke at half past six in the morning, light flooding through the uncovered skylight window and casting a warm hue across the cramped and sparsely furnished room. Not long after, I heard the clang of strong boots on the metal staircase, as others on the floor below me left the building. I guessed Kingussie would be a popular stopover for walkers, so I was glad I wasn't facing a gruelling day of hiking and such an early start as my unseen fellow residents might be.

I got up about an hour or so later and, following the recommendation from check-in, had a shower in the slightly grubby women's bathroom – the only thing to differentiate it from the men's being a couple of Monet prints on the wall.

Once dressed, I headed the short distance up the street to the little Coop supermarket, to buy some cereal bars and fruit for breakfast. Walking back, I was surprised to see, out of the corner of my eye, a man cross the road in period costume. At first glance I could see he was in a smart red uniform, reminiscent perhaps of a Jacobite-era government soldier. I looked back again just a second later and he'd disappeared. This was odd. Was he from a historical re-enactment group? Or some tourist venue? If so I had seen no evidence of it in my wanderings so far.

Left to reflect on this little mystery, I thought about the morning ahead. My train to Newtonmore was not until lunchtime, giving me a few more hours in Kingussie. I'd done the centre of the town to death the previous evening, and the forest walks up the hill too.

However, while Kingussie was largely to be found on this side of the railway line, two key sites I had in mind were a little beyond the other side of town. One was the Ruthven Barracks, a ruined eighteenth century fort, and the other was The Dell, the home of the famous Kingussie camanachd club.

All packed up and checked out, I slung my bag over my shoulders and headed off to begin properly my second day's adventures. On my way to crossing the railway line I stopped in at the railway station, to use up one of my vouchers for a journey the following day – Dalwhinnie to Blair Atholl. On many of the shorter legs on the trip, I would anticipate not seeing a conductor on board, meaning I wouldn't be able to buy a ticket, and thus saving myself a few pounds here and there. At about half an hour, however, Dalwhinnie to Blair

Atholl would be one of the longest stetches, so not an occasion to bank on avoiding a conductor.

I turned down the road over the railway line, following signs for Ruthven Barracks, looking out for the camanachd club on my way.

Shinty, as "camanachd" translates from Gaelic, is an ancient Scottish sport. It is derived from the closely-related Irish game hurling which, like the Gaelic language itself, was brought over to Scotland from Ireland many centuries ago. Not dissimilar to hockey but with considerably more physical contact permitted, shinty is a fast-paced game where injuries from high sticks or fast balls are not uncommon. It was once a widespread game. It was even played in many parts of England by Scottish exiles, and a number of English football clubs, including Nottingham Forest, were actually founded by shinty players. Over the years the game's stronghold was reduced to small pockets of the southern Highlands.

Kingussie and neighbouring club Newtonmore were two of Scotland's top teams and had long dominated the game. Indeed, Kingussie, due to their considerable success in the game, was acknowledged in 2005 by the Guinness Book of Records as the most successful sports team in the world in terms of consecutive wins. Not bad for an outfit playing in a game that is entirely amateur and receives very little public funding, commercial sponsorship or media attention. As such, I reckoned Kingussie's ground would be one of the more notable sights of the town and thus worth a quick look.

In the Uists, where I grew up, football had been virtually the only sport played to any organised level, and there had been no recent tradition of shinty.

I'd only ever seen a live shinty match once. That was in London, of all places. A few years ago I visited friends there on holiday, realising from the news just a few days beforehand that London's first shinty match for eighty years was due to be held while I was in town. Persuading a couple of friends to join me on a long trek to a sports field on the west of the city, we witnessed what was hoped to be the rebirth of London Camanachd. The newly reconstituted club took on and beat the shinty team of the Highlanders army regiment. It was good fun to watch – fast-paced, exciting and skilful.

To my shame, I'd not been to see another shinty match since. That said, London Camanachd was just one part of a continued resurgence of the game south of the border that even saw a club established in Cornwall. In 2013 a shinty match took place in the town of St Andrews between England and the USA, the first known international fixture not to involve Scotland.

Heading along the quiet road out of the village, I arrived at The Dell, Kingussie Camanachd's ground. It was empty, with just a couple of dog walkers doing a circuit around the outside of the pitch. One passed me, and his dog leapt up enthusiastically to greet me with a lot more interest than in the ball its owner was trying to throw for it. Big nets lay on the ground behind each goal, presumably to catch missed shots, but it was a mystery to me as to how they were hooked on to the huge poles that stood there.

It was a pretty setting, the cloud-topped mountains in the distance and the overcast sky creating a suitably brooding Highland scene. The ground was quiet, modest and, apart from the rather grand metal gates at the entrance featuring the club's logo, it would be easy to pass without noticing. Yet within the small world of shinty it was a site of huge significance.

Having completed my circumference of The Dell, I headed on along the road. It rose to cross the river Spey by way of a single-track nineteenth century bridge, before itself being bridged by the A9 – the main trunk road through the Highlands that forged roughly the same route as the railway line to Perth. The road took me up a gentle incline and I passed what appeared to be some old stables that had been converted into self-catering cottages, and then another short walk round to the left brought me to my destination, a landmark visible from the train: Ruthven Barracks.

The fort sat on a hill that was suspiciously smooth and even all around. The barracks being a military fort, I assumed that it would have been a constructed hill, engineered to ensure maximum protection. Yet there were plenty hills to choose from – indeed I was walking across the edge of one as I looped round toward the barracks – and so if they really wanted a natural hill for a fort then there were better choices than to construct one at great effort.

Approaching the barracks, it was remarkable to see the structure more or less intact apart from the roof: a shell, proud but hollow except for its memories. An interpretation by the side of the road, from where there were good photo opportunities not only of the barracks but back to the town too, said that, amazingly, and despite appearances, the hill was in fact natural. Formed by glacial activity, the smooth and even sides of the hill seemed impossibly perfect.

The interpretation also made mention of the former village of Ruthven, which had stood somewhere in the area, but of which "little visible trace now remains" since Kingussie was created. It was eerie and poignant to think of the arrival of the planned town of Kingussie effectively wiping a previous settlement off the map. A wave of history, lost to time.

As I climbed the hill towards the entrance of the barracks, a couple, perhaps in their late thirties, were coming out.

"Is the café open?" I joked.

"Aye, the soup's great," the man grinned back, speaking in what I took to be a Glaswegian accent.

The site of Ruthven Barracks had first been built on in the thirteenth century, and had been home to a succession of fortresses all destroyed through various conflicts. The present structure dated back to the eighteenth century, but did not enjoy a state of completeness for very long. It was built after the 1715 Jacobite rebellion, when Roman Catholic forces had first attempted to reclaim the British crown from the Protestants. The crown had changed hands at the time of 1688's so-called Glorious Revolution when William of Orange, the Dutch prince married to Mary, daughter of James II (of England and Ireland) and VII (of Scotland), claimed the throne from the Roman Catholic line of monarchs, the House of Stuart. The deposed King James was also known by the Latin name Jacob, hence the Jacobite rebellions.

The rebellions of 1715 and (more famously) 1745 had drawn on considerable support from the Highland clans, leading to the common misunderstanding that the Jacobite rebellions were a Scottish-English or Highland-Lowland schism. In fact, the mix of local clan politics, religion, money and many other factors led the situation to be a lot more complicated than that. The second Jacobite rebellion in 1745 was led by James' grandson Charles Edward Stuart, commonly known as Bonnie Prince Charlie. During the Jacobites' sweep through the Highlands, Ruthven Barracks with its garrison of government forces was besieged. After the rebellion ended at the Battle of Culloden the fort was burnt down, leaving the shell that stands today, plus the much later addition of scaffolding to support some of the walls.

I walked around the fort and spent a lot of time there, padding out my long, free morning. Birds darted in and out of the long-empty structure, and small windows provided narrowly framed views of the bleak landscape in the grey morning light. It was a tall and imposing building, even without a roof, and little sunlight penetrated the clouds and the high walls.

The large courtyard and adjacent buildings were the oldest part, according to a sign, comprising the usual elements such as soldiers' and officers' quarters, latrines, a guard house, and a prison cell. A smaller building towards the back was a later addition, in the form of stables. Strangely, there was a small wreath lying on the grass in the stables – a circular twist of what looked like heather and a fresh, pale flower like a rose. Just sitting on the ground, isolated and with no explanation, it was an odd sight. A gesture from romantic Jacobite fantasists? A memorial to someone believed to have been there as a soldier? Or maybe just a token gesture from a horse lover?

Who knows.

It was still mid-morning. I sat down on a mound inside the main courtyard, watching birds fly around. It was dry and I was sheltered by my surroundings, but it was cold. Having thoroughly explored and soaked up the atmosphere of Ruthven Barracks, there was little else for me to do in Kingussie, yet I still had plenty time before my train.

I therefore ambled as slowly as I could back from the barracks towards town. Having passed back under the A9 I saw a path marked by an RSPB sign, so I followed it into a patch of grassland stretching along the riverside. Birds sang from trees. Some horses grazed contentedly, and seemed singularly disinterested in me as I walked along the side of the gently flowing river.

I turned back after a while, and at the stile a couple of adults and three or four teenagers, were unloading canoes from a van with an outdoor centre's name on the side. They were heading for where I'd come from.

Crossing the old bridge again I turned off once more to my right, to follow a rough path along the opposite side of the river. At a bend, through some trees, I stumbled across a boy and a girl, perhaps aged fifteen or so, sitting on a low branch of a tree. We exchanged "hi"s. A few discarded beer bottles were dotted around. This was clearly a popular teenage hangout for sitting around, drinking and whatever else teenagers got up to. I was a bit conscious I'd intruded upon a quiet or possibly romantic moment, but then the soft clatter and conversation of the canoeists I'd seen earlier broke the silence as they paddled down the river. I paused to take a couple of photos of them passing, then walked on.

Returning to the road, I found a bench so I sat and had a few pieces of chocolate I had stashed away in my bag. Two jets flew loudly and low past me, shattering the serenity as they zoomed down the long glen. Although the nearest air bases were some way north at Kinloss and Lossiemouth (the former since closed in a round of defence cuts), jets were not an uncommon sight (or sound) as they undertook exercises around the Highlands.

I checked my watch again. 11:34am. Still two hours to go until my train, and I had pretty much reached the end of my "to do" list for Kingussie. I started to wonder whether I was letting myself in for an agonisingly dull week consisting of a few walks here and there, and a lot of hanging around waiting for the time to pass in places where not much happened.

For something to drag out the time, I decided to go for a final tour of Kingussie. Which, needless to say for a Tuesday mid-morning, was absolutely dead. I passed a small art gallery that opened at one o'clock. The thatched cottages of the now closed section of the Highland Folk Museum sat forlorn and decaying, just as they had yesterday. I had done as much walking around Kingussie as I could be bothered, but simply to do something I forced myself to walk back up the village's hill and round the higher streets.

As I passed the clock tower, the bell rang for noon, making me jump. It was the most noise I'd heard that morning, aside from the jets.

Deciding I was hungry, I found a butcher's down in the centre of town and bought a couple of pies. The man asked if I wanted them hot, and I said yes.

"Pies go a bit soft in the microwave," he warned me. I was a bit cold after my morning's walk, so I took the risk. They fell apart on my hands as I ate them on my amble towards the station, and while they were perfectly pleasant they were a little disappointing.

They were a metaphor for Kingussie, really.

CHAPTER 5: NEWTONMORE

My train finally arrived. At four minutes, the leg from Kingussie to Newtonmore was a short one, and just as I had expected I didn't get stopped for a ticket. The conductor did reach me, but only as we approached Newtonmore, meaning he was too busy opening the doors to check my (non-existent) ticket.

Like Carrbridge, the train line didn't cut right through the centre of Newtonmore as it did with Aviemore for instance, but skirted by some distance from it. So it was a few minutes' walk up a quiet country lane towards the main road. Passing fields of sheep and not much else made me wonder what to expect from the place. Newtonmore was one of the towns on the line I'd never been to before, and I knew nothing about it other than being home to Kingussie Camanachd's mortal enemies and the Highland Folk Museum.

First impressions were encouraging, though. I found myself on the main street, enclosed by lovely old buildings, probably around Victorian era, but which had a more homely and cheerful feel than Kingussie. I ambled down the road, keen to take my time as much as possible, and was further reassured by the Glen Hotel, whose signs boasted a good line in real ales. I noted it for a visit later.

Across the road was the Clan MacPherson museum. I was tempted to pay it a visit, but I had the Highland Folk Museum in mind as my main thing to do, and wasn't sure how much of my afternoon that would take up. Pressing on up the street, I passed the Wildcat Centre (there were many to be seen in the area, according to the information in the windows), a street sign pointing me down what seemed to be an entirely church-less Church Terrace, a hairdresser's called Maureen, and a couple of backpackers' hostels. Newtonmore seemed a whole lot more accessible and welcoming to the visitor – or maybe it was just that the sun was out and I was glad to have moved on from Kingussie.

There was a reassuringly quaint feel to Newtonmore, too. I passed a "tuck shop and café" on the main road. I'd not encountered the phrase "tuck shop" since I'd been a Cub Scout.

There was also a Coop, lots of cyclists, and the rather grand Balavil Hotel, whose upper storey windows seemed to be boarded up with upturned furniture. Either they weren't yet open for the season or they were barricading themselves in for a forthcoming zombie apocalypse. The latter eventuality was fine by me, as long as it happened five hours later once I'd left for Dalwhinnie.

My interest was piqued by a sign pointing off the main road towards Loch Imrich. According to the sign this was a circular walk, but the loch in question turned out really to be more of a large pond. Encircled by trees, it was a sedate and secluded spot tucked away from the rest of the village, the loch's calm surface broken only by the occasional duck or swan and a discarded milk carton.

I sat on a bench partway round the path and munched on a banana, enjoying the sun on my face despite some rather ominous clouds looming above.

Further around the loch there was a small shed, and an interpretation panel informed me that it was a hut used by curlers. The loch had in the past been used for curling competitions, known as bonspiels, during freezing winters. Bonspiels were obviously common occurrences back then, though less so these days since curling became an indoor sport. Two years ago there was an attempt to bring back the bonspiel near Stirling, I later discovered, but it was cancelled on safety grounds.

Despite my keenness to visit The Highland Folk Museum, which I found at the southern edge of the Newtonmore, I expected to hate it for what I predicted would be its tackiness, tweeness and stomach-churning overdose of kitsch. Scotland, not least the Highlands, has so much to offer the visitor, but all too often it is sadly reduced to a string of clichés about shortbread, tartan and simple peasants with Brigadoon accents. In this part of the world we sometimes struggle to be comfortable showing ourselves to the world, and tourist advertising seems perpetually torn between capitalising on what we're known for and trying to avoid a cringeworthy menu of clichés.

Mind you, I'm less than convinced that the reality – being overtaken by suicidally maniac drivers on the death trap that is the A9; getting soaked to the skin while going for a five-minute walk; freezing to death on a beautiful but windswept beach as you try to pretend you're enjoying yourself; arriving at a village in the middle of nowhere to find that the only tea shop closed three weeks ago; or being sprayed with spittle by a badly shaven old man who has trapped you in incomprehensible conversation in a crowded pub – is really the basis for a multimedia marketing campaign.

To my immense delight, the Highland Folk Museum was mostly tolerable in its tone, and the cheese factor was quite minimal. I was also relieved to note that the signs suggested taking three hours, which would help fill my afternoon nicely. This was because it was less a museum and actually more of a park, a vast estate with a range of period constructs and themed spaces to explore at your leisure, covering different parts of Highland life from agriculture to education to religion.

It was fairly busy when I visited, with a number of groups mostly consisting of young families and plenty of tourists.

The range of things to see was impressive. There was an early twentieth century school room, a reconstructed Victorian-era railway halt (of course erected right next to the adjacent railway line), a church, an old-fashioned post office, a garage complete with vintage tractors, and many recreated workplaces such as a weaver's house, a clockmaker's shop, a tailor's, and a grocery shop containing various old-fashioned adverts and brand names from bygone eras.

The rail halt was, naturally, of particular interest to me, sucker that I am for railway nostalgia. Hanging inside was a fading poster for the old sleeper service from Glasgow to Wick, which must have been a fun trip to take. It's easy to regard Scotland as a small country, but it's more than big enough – or the railway network slow and antiquated enough – to contain an overnight rail journey. I wonder why one doesn't still run.

The poster was titled "The First Excursion to John O'Groats And Other Places in the Land of the Never-Night". I know they were trying to make a point about the romance of a journey to those gloriously long summer days in the far north of Scotland, but the phrase "Never-Night" ended up making John O'Groats out to be some sort of zombified land of the undead. Mind you, I've been to John O'Groats. The unintended implication of the poster was not entirely wide of the mark.

It was nice to see that many of the buildings weren't just faithful copies built from scratch, but originals that had been relocated to the museum. The rail halt, for instance, had once stood further down the line at Etteridge, while the clockmaker's shop was apparently rescued from Nairn in the 1930s. I was also interested to see a sign announcing the impending arrival of the blackhouse that I'd seen lying forlornly in Kingussie. While it wasn't quite original, it was built back in 1944 and was claimed to be the oldest structure in a British open-air museum (though quite how wide the competition was in that niche field, I had no idea).

There was much to learn around the museum for the casual visitor, even though much of it – such as how a sheep fank worked – was very familiar to me from my days growing up in the Western Isles. A fank, for the uninitiated, is a concrete or metal structure, often set into the ground, in which sheep would be dipped. Dipping would usually be an annual task in which sheep get an annual bath in a whiffy cocktail of goodness knows what chemicals. We kept a small number of sheep, and would join forces with our neighbour, who had a fank, for the job of dipping. I recall almost falling into the fank once, while handling a particularly big sheep. I'm not sure what harm I'd have come to, but at least I'd have been free of tick bites for a whole year.

The museum also stuck true to the premise that no croft is complete without the remains of a rusting tractor and a randomly discarded giant kitchen sink on the ground. All that would be needed, I thought, for it to be a true Highland croft would be a three-year old copy of the West Highland Free Press sitting in a broken plastic bucket, a rotting sheep skull, and a discarded tin of Tennent's Lager rusting in a ditch.

In a replica of an early twentieth century kitchen, there was an opportunity for some interactivity, with pieces of paper set out for people to write down memories of wartime rationing. With clearly a good ear for a family story, one visitor called had written:

> "My grandpa was so looking forward to trying his first ever banana after the war. When he finally got hold of one, it was a big anticlimax. To this day, he still doesn't like bananas and has no idea what the fuss was about!
>
> Meg (aged 11)"

One in the eye there for the Banana Marketing Board.

A note in Spanish was also posted, and thanks to a helpful Spanish speaker I've learned that it translates as:

"I'm sorry, I have nothing but we were here.

Fito Omar Bea, Torrejón de Ardoz, Madrid, España"

I think we can agree that for valued contributions, Meg (aged 11) beats poor Fito from Madrid hands down.

In one recreated nineteenth century crofthouse, I found the most cringeworthy part of the museum. I was surprised to meet a woman inside, dressed in simple tweed clothing and attempting to be "authentic". I said hello and she started telling me all about the house, using the first person and the present tense – "this is our bedroom, and this is where we sleep…". I wanted to shake her by the shoulders and tell her I wasn't five years old and knew she didn't really live in the house and exist in the pre-electric age. But she was obviously so conditioned to being "in character" that I just humoured her for a few minutes before politely making my excuses and leaving.

Further to the northern end of the museum lay a collection of thatched cottages, outside one of which sat a woman in period costume knitting and being photographed by foreign tourists. I steered clear. Nearby, a sign at the beginning of a path down a slope said "Staff only beyond this point". Perhaps it was their secret little lair in the hills for when the visitors got too much for them.

I'd soon covered most of the museum, and it was time to head back into the village. I'd enjoyed the tour a lot more than I'd expected, and figured that for older children it would be fascinating. The museum boasted such a wide range of structures and periods of recent history, the kitsch factor was not as endemic as I had feared, and I had even learned one or two little things myself. Above all, it was a relief to have found such a good place to pass a couple of hours.

I had another two hours or so until my train, and my stomach told me that it was time to get some food. So I retraced my steps back through the village to the Glen Hotel, which I had seen earlier, and found a seat in their comfortable and surprisingly busy bar. I ordered a pint of Wildcat, from the Cairngorm Brewery. After a busy day's wandering around, it didn't last long. I perused the food menu, and it seemed like they did a good range of Scottish food but with refreshing twists – I ordered a pork and haggis burger. I wondered why I had never come across the idea of merging pork with haggis – two soft, flavoursome meats that went together fabulously.

I sadly couldn't linger too long, but there was time to accompany the remains of my burger with a second pint, so I went back up to the bar.

"Another Wildcat, please. That first one went down far too quickly."

I ended up getting chatting to the barman about real ales, and the impressive number they had on offer.

"We have four real ale pumps going all summer and folk love them," he said. I mentioned a few of the places in Inverness where you could get a good pint, and he told me that the Inverness Camra (Campaign for Real Ale) group was coming down to the pub a couple of months later, just to try their beers.

Some moments later, three folk went up the bar, obviously tourists.

"I'm from table nine", one of them informed the barman loudly and clearly, as if announcing his arrival from a foreign land. It sounded like basis for a comedy sketch, a balance of power situation played out in a bar, where different nations represented by different groups had to try to form peaceful trading relations by entering into kitties with friendly tables. Perhaps it would all turn into a bar-room brawl conducted as a recreation of the perilous nature of international relations.

When I went up to pay my bill after I finished eating, the barman undercharged me, forgetting my first pint. I pointed it out.

"Thanks for your honesty."

"It would have come out of his pocket," said one of the

other staff, overhearing. He said it in jest but I am sure it would have been quite true as well.

I left the hotel, well-fed and watered, and determined that for the delicious food and good beer at the Glen Hotel alone, Newtonmore was well worth a second visit. With that on top of the peaceful walk round Loch Imrich and the massive expanse of the Highland Folk Museum, the village was a veritable gem that I was sure was overlooked by far too many visitors.

I arrived down at the station to find that I was the only person on the quiet, single-platform stop. Across the lines lay the overgrown mess that was the now defunct opposite platform, with an empty field and low hills stretching out beyond. The sky was turning a dark grey, hinting at possible rain and inevitable dusk.

Just along the platform, in what would have been the old station house, a man and boy were sitting in the garden. They had slings and were doing target practice on a can and box that had been placed on fence posts on the other side of the railway line. I supposed that the building would now be a holiday cottage, and they must have been bored towards the end of their break. It was a good job they hadn't been staying in Kingussie.

An automated announcement on the station tannoy shattered the silence.

"Do not leave baggage unattended. Unattended baggage is likely to be removed without warning."

I looked round. By whom? There was no staff member at the station. There was, however, a man up in the signal box just behind the station. Although the pointless announcement was quite amusing, I figured the signalman wasn't laughing. He'd no doubt heard all the announcements. Over and over and over again. A million times. He probably woke up perspiring and demented in the middle of the night on a regular basis, screaming ferociously at the calm, clinical voices in his head telling him that this was a no smoking area or that the next train was for Edinburgh.

Talking of which, my train soon arrived, and while I was sad to be leaving Newtonmore I was delighted to be able to jump on board and rush up the carriage to the toilet just in time.

CHAPTER 6: DALWHINNIE

Just towards the end of my time in Newtonmore it had started to rain, and it continued to do so as I arrived at Dalwhinnie, the sky now nearly fully dark.

Dalwhinnie was a small village, indeed the smallest of the places I'd visited so far on the line, and so it was a short journey down the street through the rain to the bunkhouse where I'd booked accommodation.

Searching for somewhere to stay in Dalwhinnie, where I knew I would be spending the night, had been a slightly confusing task. I knew, from frequent journeys past on the train, that the village would not be groaning with accommodation options, but I was aware of a large building at the south of the village, quite some distance back from the train line, that looked rather like a hotel.

I found reference to a couple of hotel names on the internet, but it wasn't quite clear whether that indicated two hotels, or just the same establishment that had changed hands or gained a new name. What was clear, however, was a large number of pretty unappealing online reviews of one of the names, with the customer service and food coming in for particular criticism.

Thankfully, though, my searches led me to the website of a

cheap and basic bunkhouse. The tone of its website suggested it was a cosy and friendly place, so I booked in.

When I arrived, a man in perhaps his late fifties was just coming out of a door.

"Is this the bunkhouse?" I asked.

"You must be Stephen."

"Simon," I corrected. I'd had a phone call from them earlier in the afternoon asking what time I'd be arriving. It was an eerily familiar error, as Stephen is the name of my brother and I was mistakenly called it many times through childhood. The thought that the man at the bunkhouse had been stalking the entire Varwell clan for many years was dismissed in my head as rather less likely than simply being confused between two similar sounding names.

He introduced himself as Ron, and he along with his wife owned and managed the bunkhouse. He had just been feeding three Polish fencing workers who were staying there.

"So brush up on your Polish. I'll have to be up to give them breakfast at six thirty."

"It doesn't have to be six thirty for me, does it?" I asked, in horror.

"No, of course not!" Ron said with a smile. We settled on a much more civilised eight o'clock. My onward train was about eleven o'clock and I wanted to try to take in the village's distillery first thing in the morning.

He showed me to my room, through a door into what was clearly an older part of the premises, and into a carpeted hallway. There was a homely, if slightly faded, feel to the place, and the room I was in had a bunk bed with a double on the bottom and single on top. I had the room to myself, according to Ron, which was just as it had been the previous night in Kingussie. That, I suppose, was one advantage of travelling long before the peak of the tourist season.

"Dzień dobry", I said to one of the Poles who appeared in the corridor, a young, thin guy with a mop of dark hair. In a tone of mild surprise, he replied with a sentence in which I recognised the word "polska".

"No, I'm Scottish," I said, guessing his question. "That's all the Polish I know, though."

In the years following Poland's entry into the European Union, Inverness had, like many places in Britain, acquired a large Polish population and the language was a familiar sound on the streets of the city. I was pleased that my pronunciation of the one phrase I knew in the language was convincing enough to make the man ask if I was Polish.

"You have a good room," he said, nodding towards my door. "Double bed. I was in there a couple of weeks ago."

"Sorry to steal your favourite," I said with a grin.

"OK," he said with a humourless shrug. "Not your decision." My Polish pronunciation was clearly better than my ability to convey deadpan humour.

I flopped on to the bed to put my feet up and munch a bag of crisps I'd bought earlier, and I wondered what I would do for the remainder of the evening. I contemplated going for a walk, and perhaps seeing if the hotel with dodgy reviews had a bar to sit and have a pint in. It would, I imagined, be either a delightful place crammed full of celebratory hillwalkers, fine ales and toe-tapping live music, or a farcical experience to rival the worst of Fawlty Towers. I was tired, it was dark and raining, and I'd already had two pints with my dinner in Newtonmore. But I figured that there was no harm in a wee nightcap. I picked up my jacket and headed out.

I was glad to find that the rain had eased as I headed down the road again. I stopped at a T-junction where a community notice board stood. Pride of place was given to a large multilingual poster offering confidential advice to victims of domestic abuse. There were also adverts for a Buddhist meditation and talk, and for a series of Lent classes. Highly spiritual, but prone to violence: was Dalwhinnie the Jerusalem of the Highland Line?

I turned right at the junction. I was now walking parallel to the railway line, heading south on what would once have been the main road prior to the A9's construction. The A9 itself was some distance over to my left, a shadowy presence on my journey so far and never too far from the route of the railway line. The gentle hum of traffic was the only noise I could hear as I headed towards where I remembered from past train journeys the hotel should be. A bolt of light shooting along the railway line penetrated the stillness and darkness. The last train south, I figured.

Further down the road, some lights gave shape in the gloom to a camp of temporary cabins, seemingly some sort of building site. "Balfour Beatty" was written on the side of most of the cabins. I recognised the name as a big construction company. There was no evidence of what they were building, but whatever it was required a large effort.

I heard a curlew call out in the dark. Jupiter hung bright in the sky against a starry backdrop. A dark blue aura over the hills to the west, the very last vestiges of daylight, and the soft orange glow of the occasional streetlight were all the illumination to be had. Directly behind me, at the other end of the village, I could see the lights of the distillery, tomorrow morning's destination.

Eventually I arrived at the hotel, at least judging by the very small "hotel car park" sign. But strangely there was no sign indicating the hotel's name, nor any lights on. It was standing abandoned and lifeless in the darkness.

Except, curiously, for a van and a car, both sporting Specsavers logos on the side. A handful of men and women in smart business attire were lifting bags of luggage. I continued to watch, and what was particularly odd at this late hour was that they weren't arriving, but seemingly loading their bags into the backs of the vehicles. The two vehicles pulled off, heading north, leaving me alone to ponder on the strangeness of a Specsavers staff convention outside an empty, lifeless hotel.

I walked on a bit more and reached a petrol station, closed up and in darkness. It was the end of the village as far as I could see. I turned back, past the ghostly hotel and the Balfour Beatty site, and back to the bunkhouse.

If there was any nightlife in Dalwhinnie, I thought to myself as I sat on my bed eating the rest of my crisps, this was it. And, of course, the Poles watching television down the corridor.

It was just as well. It was ten o'clock and I had an early start the next morning. Admittedly not as early as for the Poles, but after a day of lots of walking around Kingussie, Newtonmore and now here, I could do with going to bed.

I slept deeply, and woke the next morning to the sound of the Poles leaving the building, meaning I could go back to sleep for another hour. Comfortingly, the heater was powering away and the room was lovely and warm.

Ron greeted me when I went in to the main restaurant area, a large space with a long bar and lots of tables. It was all very modern and bright, but without feeling cold or unwelcoming, and Ron got cooking while Radio 2 played in the background.

After eating my large and delicious cooked breakfast, I packed my bag and returned to check out. As I did so, Ron asked if I was hillwalking. I said no and explained what my journey was all about.

I complemented Ron on what a lovely place the bunkhouse was, and he told me a bit about it. The big, bright restaurant and reception area we were standing in was a modern extension to the small remaining part of a 1930s hotel, an apparently lovely building that had been mostly destroyed due to concrete cancer (an affliction of which I had never heard). Where we stood, he said, was a combination of the old bar, offices and a cocktail bar.

I took the opportunity of this chatty local to resolve a couple of the previous night's mysteries, and asked first about the Balfour Beatty camp. It was, Ron replied, the base for the central section of the Beauly-Denny power line. That was the huge and controversial chain of electricity pylons being built down the middle of Scotland from Beauly near Inverness to Denny in the Central Belt. The chain of huge pylons, bigger than any that Scotland had seen before, was crucial (so claimed its advocates) to fully connect the rapidly increasing network of renewable energy generation such as wind power in the north of Scotland with the bulk of Scotland's population in the south. Opinion, including even that within the environmental movement, was bitterly divided, but after protracted debate the line was finally going ahead. I realised I must have heard of Balfour Beatty in amongst all the news reporting of the controversial project over the past months.

"Many of the workers stay out at the camp of course, but I get a few in here, so it keeps business going," Ron went on. "Mostly it's hillwalkers we get, but we're the only place in town since the hotel down the road closed a few years ago."

"I was going to ask about that too," I said. "I walked past it last night and it was all closed up."

"Well, the hotel had been owned latterly by a couple from down south," Ron explained, "who arrived with all sorts of inappropriate ideas that were never going to work up here. The wife and kids left the man after a while. He wasn't a nice chap and was totally unsuited to the hospitality trade if I can put it that way.

"One time, two families were in having dinner. The man from one family went up to the bar to tell the owner the food was awful. The owner angrily leapt over the counter and grabbed him, whereupon the man from the other family calmly got up and produced a warrant card – he was an off-duty police officer!"

As Ron described it, the policeman dragged the owner outside and "read him the riot act". Ron wasn't quite sure what happened next, but the next day the owner apparently disappeared to the USA for three months.

"The problem was, he never left the heating or the water on, and it was the first of the big bad winters a few years ago. He came back to find the hotel ruined. He's not around any more.

"Since then the place has been broken into, stripped, vandalised, the copper's all gone… it's a shame. It needs half a million pounds of work done, and who's got that these days?"

Like the bunkhouse, the hotel had been a mix of the old and new. It was mostly a modern place, Ron told me, but the oldest part was built by Wade, the British General who had been involved in putting down the 1715 Jacobite rebellion and who later on led work on building roads, bridges and other infrastructure throughout the Highlands – largely for the benefit of the military.

With the hotel now out of action, Ron was working hard to get the bunkhouse fully up and running. He was a community councillor, he said, and was conscious that as the only hostel or eatery in the village it was important to make it work. He had plans to make it a social enterprise so everyone in the community had a stake in it. Ron spoke with such enthusiasm and passion for the project. He himself had an accent that I took to be from somewhere in the north of England, demonstrating that, unlike the unpleasant man who had led the hotel to ruin, it was perfectly possible for folk to come up to the Highlands from the south and make a good go of things.

Our conversation came abruptly to an end as two people, perhaps tourists, came in for breakfast. I said thank you and goodbye to Ron and headed off.

It was inspiring to have met someone striving to make a go of the bunkhouse. It was a great position to be in as the only place like it in the village, and with such good hillwalking in the area it would be a valuable stopover for many people. That said, it was clearly hard work. Good luck to him, I thought to myself as I hit the road once more.

I had a couple of hours or so until my train, and so my plan was to visit the only other major commercial venture in the village – the Dalwhinnie distillery. As it sat right next to the railway line, I'd seen it in passing many times, and it rather dominated the landscape, a big complex of white buildings at the top of a gentle hill a short walk out of town.

I knew – collector as I am of totally useless facts – that it was the highest working distillery in Scotland in terms of altitude. There was a higher distillery (Braeval, in Speyside) but that had long been closed down. Apparently, though, production at Braeval had recently recommenced, meaning it would reclaim the title from Dalwhinnie.

It was a cold and crisp morning, the lightest of frosts on the ground and a smattering of snow on the hilltops that stood out boldly against the blue sky. It took me just a few minutes to walk to the distillery, and I discovered that I was a little too early for the visitor centre opening, so I sat at a wooden picnic table and wrote up some notes for a bit. There was a strong, sickly sweet smell of whisky. It would have been lovely later on in the day, but at this early hour of the morning it was somewhat overbearing.

While at university I worked in a distillery for a summer as a tour guide, and it confirmed my love of whisky. The craftsmanship throughout the whole process was a wonder in itself, and the end product was of course sublime. Whenever I visited distilleries since then I always enjoyed detecting the subtle differences in the smells between each corresponding stage of the process. Of course the basic production process was more or less the same wherever the distillery was, meaning that the variation came down to details such as the type of yeast, the character of the water, or the wood used in the barrels.

In time, I saw two people in what looked like distillery uniform walking towards the door of the visitor centre, and they noticed me as approached them. It turned out that, although it was nearly half past nine and thus opening time, there wasn't actually a tour until ten o'clock. I explained I had half an eye on the time due to having a train to catch, and so one of them – who introduced himself as Brian – said he would take me round earlier on something of a speeded up tour. It looked like I was the only visitor at the time, so I would enjoy a tour all to myself.

Of course I knew the gist of whisky production quite well, so when I mentioned my old summer job Brian kindly glossed over the generalities and focussed instead on the particular characteristics of Dalwhinnie.

For instance, I'd always wondered why Dalwhinnie produced nothing younger than a fifteen year old single malt, when many other distilleries would produce a ten or twelve year old. Brian explained that this was due to Dalwhinnie's high altitude. In the thinner and colder air, evaporation was a slower process and it took those extra few years of maturation to make the whisky the required quality.

Another neat feature Brian pointed out was how old-fashioned stills – the giant copper pots used in the distilling stage – used to have a little window at the top so the stillmen could look inside and see how things were doing. It was a dangerous task as you'd need to climb a ladder up the side of the still, which was not only very tall but also made of metal and thus extremely hot. The stills at Dalwhinnie, however, were a modern type and had in-built cameras to monitor the whisky.

It made me think of Cheddarvision, an internet phenomenon from a few years ago. A cheese factory in England had decided to install a webcam to film one of its cheeses as it sat maturing in a warehouse. It was clearly a light-hearted public relations stunt, but it was an unexpected hit. Cheddarvision received hundreds of thousands of views and a growing band of hardcore fans, who apparently got quite excited when, at one point, it looked like the cheese's label was slowly peeling off. If you hunt around on YouTube, you can see a speeded up video of its year-long maturation. Gripping stuff, I'm sure you'll agree. I mentioned this to Brian, and we both agreed that Distillevision had the potential to be a hit too.

On such a one-to-one tour Brian and I inevitably got talking on a more personal level. He lived in Aviemore, he told me, but had to give up a job there due to an injury. Now he commuted to Dalwhinnie.

Aviemore!

It seemed like such a distant memory to me. It was only about half an hour from Aviemore to Dalwhinnie by car or train, yet on my slow journey I had left there the day before yesterday.

The conclusion of the tour, naturally, was a dram of the fifteen year old. It was a lovely, sweet whisky with a warm and ever so slightly peaty aftertaste. I bought a small bottle of it in the shop, and Brian gave me a voucher for free tours in various other distilleries across the country that were owned by the same company. Such is the modern world, that a trade that portrays itself as a timeless continuation of an ancient craft is actually awash with global brands that tend to own a range of big names in the alcohol industry. Dalwhinnie was owned by one such brand. One of the other distilleries on the voucher was Blair Athol, and my next stop was the village of the same name.

Slowly I walked back through the village to the railway station, the weather still bright and surprisingly warm, which was an encouraging sign for the rest of the day. I had the small, unmanned station to myself, though there was not much to see other than the empty, locked room through the window of the station building. It contained a shiny white fridge and a plastic bin, so obviously station staff did base themselves there occasionally, perhaps for maintenance work. There was a no smoking sign on the wall, along with a poster portraying two rats and exhorting people to dispose of food properly.

On the outside of the building was a small plaque that Ron at the bunkhouse had told me to look out for. Dated the fifteenth of May 2004, it commemorated the sixtieth anniversary of a visit by General (later Field marshal) Montgomery, one of the leaders of British forces during the Second World War.

"General Montgomery stayed in Dalwhinnie in his special train Rapier, for a four-day rest period during his planning of the D-Day landings"

the plaque said. It went on to quote his last words to villagers as he departed:

"Thank you for the welcome to Dalwhinnie, I am grateful for

having been left in peace and quiet and have enjoyed my holiday. Now I must go off and see if we can get this war finished."

Monty's words did come over as rather grumpy, making the good folk of Dalwhinnie sound like the sort of people that you really want to leave you alone. But I guess he had bigger things on his mind at that particular moment in time.

As I waited, two young women and two toddlers were dropped off by a car, along with some huge suitcases. We exchanged hellos, the tranquility of this sleepy little station shattered as the two women began chatting animatedly to each other.

One of the women got a text message, and read it out to the other, and it seemed to be something about having had a lovely weekend. Judging by their accents, they were from somewhere in the south of England. It would be a long journey home for them from wherever they were staying. Much longer than mine, of course, even though I was about to undertake one of the longest legs of my trip – twenty-five minutes to Blair Atholl.

The train soon arrived, and I helped the women with their suitcases while they carried the children on board.

As we pulled out of the station I saw on the right hand side a grand old house sitting by the side of a loch that I had so often seen and wondered about. The water was, as I've since discovered, Loch Ericht. Meanwhile the house was An Tochailt, a lodge rentable by the public. Built of a sharp, angular granite it exuded a proud Victorian grandeur, and managed to look both relatively modern and evocative of ancient castles at the same time. Had I had more time on my journey I would have gladly gone for a walk along the paths on either side of the loch.

When I'd originally begun planning the trip, some months previously, Dalwhinnie had been an important hinge on which my entire schedule depended. The consecutive villages of Newtonmore, Dalwhinnie and Blair Atholl were three of the line's smaller and less frequently served stopping points. There was only one train a day from Newtonmore to Dalwhinnie, which ran mid-morning, so I was tied to taking it. However the next train from there to Blair Atholl was in the early evening, giving me eight hours to kill in Dalwhinnie. My first thought was to plan a hike into the hills, but I didn't want to stray too far out of the village – again, my trip was about looking at the towns and villages along the line, not the wider areas. Plus, I didn't want to be weighed down by serious hillwalking gear that I would almost certainly not use anywhere else along the journey.

Rather concerned at the prospect of spending eight hours in a village where I knew there was little to do (there would only so many times I could do a tour of the distillery, for instance), my second idea was to follow the tracks along Loch Ericht.

However, my plans changed when the timetables were updated and it turned out that I would need to stay overnight in Dalwhinnie instead. Unless I'd sacrificed the distillery tour, there would have been insufficient daylight to take the fairly long walk out of the village and down to the lodge.

So it was yet another fleeting glimpse of Loch Ericht from a train window as I headed south once more. It was something to come back for another time.

CHAPTER 7: BLAIR ATHOLL

A short while out of Dalwhinnie, the line followed a river southwards, with the A9 close by on our left and hills rising up on either side. I saw a rickety wooden bridge swung low over the river, presumably providing access for walkers. At its lowest point it was just a metre or so above the water, but it was not fixed to anything other than posts at either end. The wooden slats looked so fragile and the metal chain providing the handrails seemed so disarmingly slack, that care would be required when walking over. If the bridge had been at a more substantial height, it would have been worthy of a scene from an Indiana Jones film.

My journey from Dalwhinnie to Blair Atholl, through empty and desolate terrain, was something of a milestone. The rugged mountains that encircled Dalwhinnie gave way to softer shapes and lusher colours further south. From bare and dramatic mountainsides to expansive, green forests, this was a definite change from the Highlands to Perthshire. I felt like I was starting to make substantial progress on my adventure.

This stretch of the line was a very sparsely populated part of the world – even by Highlands standards. The train would pass through no settlements between Dalwhinnie and Blair Atholl, the only signs of life being the A9, the occasional house, and the tourist trap that was the House of Bruar, an overpriced shop and restaurant that sold all the tartan tat that kitsch-hunting coach tours could dream of.

It was arguably, however, the prettiest leg of my journey, taking in the southern limits of the Cairngorm mountains and the Drumochter Pass which, at four hundred and sixty-one metres, was the highest point of not just the Highland Main Line but the entire British rail network.

The journey was marred only by the fact that I didn't see a conductor, meaning the £9.90-worth of vouchers I had spent on buying a ticket for this leg back in Kingussie had been in vain.

I arrived at Blair Atholl, a pretty village of mostly Victorian-era stone but some older buildings too, with a lot more of an experience of the place than I had for most of the previous stops. Being more or less halfway to the central belt, Nicole and I had stopped here a handful of times on the occasions we'd driven south. Like every town on the A9 between Inverness and Perth, Blair Atholl is bypassed. But sometimes we would turn off and stop for a drink. Our destination would either be the Atholl Arms Hotel, the epitome of slightly faded small town hotel grandeur, or the delightful Watermill café, a opportunity to grab a bite at a working grain mill, a centuries-old building that was one of the last remaining functioning water mills in the country.

The only other place of note in the village related to the fact that Blair Atholl owed its existence – and its name – to one person. No, not Lionel Blair, but the Duke of Atholl. Or, to be precise, the Dukes of Atholl, a title that dated back to 1703.

The most significant building in the village was Blair Castle, home to the many generations of dukes. It lay to the east of the main road that ran through the village, hiding behind the protection of thick trees, a vast piece of land, and a stone wall that flanked the length of the left side of the road if you headed south through the village. The rest of the village lay to the right.

The dukes were actors in a long and eventful stretch of history. They owned Britain's only legal private army, the Atholl Highlanders, a regiment of the British army that was disbanded in the eighteenth century only to be resurrected some years later by one of the dukes as a private bodyguard. Perhaps a bodyguard was a good idea, because the dukes were not universally loved – they were among the chief protagonists of the Highland Clearances, when thousands of people were brutally cleared by landowners across the north of Scotland in the eighteenth and nineteenth centuries.

The Atholl Highlanders were also used as a ceremonial guard on the occasions of royal visits, which were not as rare as you might think in this part of the world. The nineteenth century saw two developments that contributed to the village's royal influence: the coming of the railways, and the building of Balmoral Castle, the royal residence on Deeside. As such, Blair Atholl made for a short detour for Queen Victoria en route to her Highland home, where she could pop in and visit her aristocratic friend (and, one can probably assume, distant relative) the duke.

The castle was a beautiful place, as the occasional fleeting glimpses of the grand, gleaming white structure from the train or car would demonstrate. However, for me the real interest was the village itself, much more obvious and evident from the train, and given I had only three hours there I didn't want to waste the better part of it on a castle tour, however interesting that might be. Plus, at nine pounds the entry fee was somewhat prohibitive.

One thought was to do the tour of the old water mill. I'd been to the café, of course, but never toured the working part of the mill. Another idea was to try to track down the Blair Athol distillery, for which I had a voucher following my Dalwhinnie distillery tour. I had assumed it must be in or near Blair Atholl, albeit that the distillery, curiously, spelled Athol with one 'l', but there was no sign of it anywhere. Admittedly I'd never heard of it or seen it on my few trips through the village, and I was not certain it was even in Blair Atholl itself, but it was surely a reasonable guess. It was strange, then, to find no evidence on the maps at the small, quaint Victorian station when I arrived, nor any mention on signposts.

To begin my exploration of Blair Atholl, I headed north along the only road through the village, past many of its finest buildings. They included the Atholl House Hotel and the village church, a pleasant if uninspiring building surrounded by a graveyard. It was a relatively warm and calm day, and I spotted a duck sitting on one of the graves, sunning itself. I wondered whether, in an anatine twist on the Greyfriars Bobby story, it was the beloved pet of one of the deceased.

Beyond that lay The Atholl Country Life Museum, which looked like a useful place to spend an hour or two. A relatively small museum, it had the statue of a white horse over the door, which, according to the sign outside, used to stand atop the Atholl Arms Hotel. Though there was no explanation as to why it had moved. There was nobody at the museum's front desk, so I just opened the inner door and went in.

Despite its compact size, the museum was a veritable treasure trove of local history and was packed almost literally to the rafters with artefacts on many different aspects of local life and history. From an exhibit on "Atholl's unsung hero", a soldier called Donald MacBeath who fought in the Crimean War and whose great grandfather fought at Culloden, to a sleigh used by a doctor in the village in the early twentieth century to transport patients in the snow, via a 1902 picture of Glen Bruar, "the most impressive Highland pony stallion of his time", it was an eclectic portrait of the area's past.

Inevitably, there was plenty on the Dukes of Atholl too, including John George, the eighth duke, who apparently conceived of the idea of the Scottish National War Memorial and was one of the brains behind the Forestry Commission.

There were also rooms from a period house, a reconstructed Post Office, information on everything from the railways to Gaelic to peat, and much more. But perhaps my favourite exhibit was the wooden frame used to paint the first white lines on the village's roads. If there exists a more wonderfully parochial celebration of the banal in any museum anywhere on earth, I'd love to hear about it.

My route through the cosy little museum involved passing through the conversation of a group of people who seemed to be having a meeting – presumably staff or volunteers. I asked if it was okay to pass by and I was very happily waived on. A man, perhaps of retirement age, followed me into the next room and we got talking. He mentioned, very politely, that the museum was actually closed.

I apologised profusely – I'd not seen a sign, and the door was open so I thought it would be OK to just go in – but the man insisted I'd be welcome to look around. He asked about where I was from and I explained the nature of my trip.

Quite taken by this, he made a point of showing me the exhibits about the railway line. He explained that the following year, 2013, would be the one hundred and fiftieth anniversary of the Highland Main Line's completion, and they were planning a big showcase for the occasion.

Back through in the main room, I got talking to two ladies from the meeting I had clearly interrupted, and they also asked what I was doing in Blair Atholl.

"Well, you'll not be stopping at Killiecrankie, Struan, Dalnaspidal…"

They began chatting about all the closed stations on this part of the line, more victims of the Beeching Axe. The man who I'd first spoken to said that there were seventy people working at Blair Atholl station once upon a time. With all the old local stations children would often take the train to school, including himself: "the ten to nine to Pitlochry", he remembered.

There was clearly a lot of work put into the museum by the volunteers, and it was a real community effort with many people involved. The man stressed to me that it "wasn't just a case of putting stuff in a box", either: there were many stages to go through including planning, interpretation, preparation, cataloguing, computer imaging, and of course presentation.

So many small museums – and, frankly, too many big ones – are rubbish. This one therefore was a surprisingly informative experience, all the more impressive for being run by such a dedicated team of local enthusiasts.

Thanking the folk for all their information, and apologising again for intruding when they were closed, I left them to the rest of their meeting and headed out again.

Nearly at the top of the village, I went over the river and found myself in the Bridge of Tilt, a tiny village presumably fated to be the forgotten twin, or more likely the runty little brother, to the comparative metropolis of Blair Atholl. There was a path through trees immediately over the bridge on my left, though I figured I wasn't so desperate to fill time that I needed to go on yet another forest walk. I'd had more than enough of those in the various stops so far.

Among the few buildings in the Bridge of Tilt was the tourist information centre, which I thought was curiously out of the way. Even odder, given it was the Easter holidays, I found it was closed. There was also no mention of the elusive Blair Athol distillery among the notices in the window.

After returning to Blair Atholl proper, I took a look around the water mill museum, which was basically a sign-posted walkthrough of the mill's production process. One of the last water mills in Scotland, there had been milling on the site since the late sixteenth century. Interpretations throughout the old building told of the process and history of the place, and how they used their own flour in the café's baking.

That the mill was made entirely from wooden equipment, despite having lived as such through an era of industrialisation, struck me as strange. It looked fake, not least in its pristine condition and with the immaculate wooden floors. There had, I assumed, been renovations and replacements over the years so this was presumably not the originally sixteenth century equipment they were still using. The building was clearly old, but the machinery looked like it could have been assembled just yesterday. Nevertheless it was a beautiful and no doubt complex piece of work.

Avoiding the temptation of the watermill's excellent café, which I had visited a number of times before, I slowly ambled across the main road and followed signs to the Blair Castle estate office. Even though I wasn't visiting the castle I did want to see if I could get a good photo of it without paying to get in. Thanks to the thick trees encircling the castle there was no such luck. In any case, it was not long before my next train, so I wandered back to the station.

After my exploration of Blair Atholl I was quite tired, though there were still two places left to see that day before I would finish the day in Perth.

There were echoes around the station of what the man in the museum had said about it having been a busier site in the past. Though the station was quiet, it was quite large. A bricked up doorway on wall of the station building spoke of past comings and goings. A once teeming place, I now had it to myself.

Along the platform, a sign read:

"Public Telephone
For details of the nearest telephone, please consult the station information poster."

Intrigued by this pointless waste of words, I searched in vain on the platform for the poster itself, let alone the actual phone in question. Had I found the poster, I imagined it would have been consistently Kafkaesque and simply referred me on elsewhere for details of the phone. Perhaps the nightmare would end up requiring a notice that read:

"For details of the poster about the station information poster that contains details of the nearest telephone, please consult the station station station information poster poster poster."

Soon bored with musings on a perpetual hell of public information, I climbed the steps of the station footbridge and took my now obligatory photo down the line. Much like with previous stations, it gave for a tranquil shot – empty platforms, and trees lining the track on either side. Green, brown and purple colours covered the hillsides; blue, white and grey shades blanketed the sky.

Silence.

The line curved away round the corner, southwards, towards where I would be heading next.

CHAPTER 8: PITLOCHRY

"Just a single?" asked the conductor, with a note of surprise at my desire to travel the eleven-minute journey in only one direction. His mild but polite inquisitiveness was the closest any conductor on my journey got to querying the oddness of my ticket requests – even on those legs of just a minute or two. "Three pounds seventy," he replied to my affirmation.

The train passed one of the most spectacular parts of the journey, the Pass of Killiecrankie, where the train enters a short tunnel and then bursts on to a magnificent stretch running along the top of the pass, a break in the trees allowing for a lovely view of the steep, forested hillside across the water and the run of the river below along the length of the pass. It's a stunning spot, though frustrating for its brevity. You often see tourists reach in delight for their cameras only for the moment to pass just as quickly. One day, I'll head down to the river somehow and get some nice shots of the deep gorge and the trains passing by at the top.

At Pitlochry I had just under two hours. This, uniquely, dipped under my minimum limit, but given the logistics of subsequent legs of the journey it was the only viable option. In any case, I knew Pitlochry moderately, also due to a number of stops on road journeys. While Blair Atholl was our preferred stop southbound for a coffee when heading away to see family, a chippy in Pitlochry was one of our favourite stops on our return trips late in the day.

It was a bustling tourist town, one of the places on the line that turned into an important Victorian-era tourist destination when the railways came. There was a prim and proper air about the place, with immaculate shops on the main street selling overpriced jumpers and posh fudge, and the huge Atholl Palace hotel. Through the occasional gap in the trees, this giant of a castle with elegant spires could be seen from the train line, atop a hill looking out over the village. It was one of many grand places in this evidently very proud town. It was also seemingly a good place to retire to – large adverts for retirement flats were one of the first things you saw as trains from the north approached the station.

Although I'd stopped in Pitlochry at least a handful of times, I'd never really explored that deeply. But with little desire to browse through the numerous touristy shops in the town, I wasn't totally sure what I would do. However, when I undertook my customary consultation of the map at the station, I found my answer – the Blair Athol Distillery.

So that explained its mysterious absence in Blair Atholl! I checked again the voucher that I'd got at Dalwhinnie and decided I couldn't go wrong with a free tour of a distillery to spend some time. So I wondered down the road, past shops selling sickeningly expensive knitwear and crafts, past a cute little chapel just out of the main hub of the village, past a neat little square with a war memorial, and arrived at the distillery. Dark grey stone buildings with ivy growing up the walls greeted me.

Sadly it turned out that I could indeed go wrong with a free tour of a distillery.

The experience back at Dalwhinnie had been an intimate and friendly one, where I'd been the only customer and I'd had the undivided attention of Brian the knowledgeable and friendly tour guide.

Here at the Blair Athol distillery, in contrast, it was a major operation and a busy tourist attraction. I found myself surrounded by busloads of tourist groups, and was one of about thirty people being led around the path of the tour. In amongst the noise of other people and, at times, the huge machinery, it was really hard to hear the guide, who wasn't marshalling people well or speaking anywhere near loudly enough.

The whisky at the end of the tour wasn't especially memorable either, and certainly not as good as the Dalwhinnie.

Perhaps my grumpy mood was exacerbated by the fact I was tired. I was, after all, well into my third day of what was turning into one inordinately long, steady walk.

I walked back to the railway station, content that I'd seen enough of Pitlochry to know it might be worth another explore (the distillery aside). I had just a bit of time to spare, which allowed me a few minutes in the pokey and very busy bookshop that occupied part of the station building, the shelves of which I would see through its window when passing by on the train. I appreciated seeing it from the inside for once, but I had neither time nor inclination for a purchase.

I also needed to visit the ticket office to use one of my vouchers to buy a ticket and there was a bit of a wait at the counter. The problem was one individual, a middle aged woman who seemed to be taking an inordinate amount of time to explain the nature of a complaint she had about a previous journey.

Eventually, with the minutes and seconds ticking by, it was my turn. But in the midst of my query – over which the man behind the counter was taking a phenomenally long time over what should have been a simple transaction – the train arrived. So I just cancelled my request, took my money and the voucher, and left, figuring I could use the voucher the next day.

CHAPTER 9: DUNKELD AND BIRNAM

My journey of just under fifteen minutes took me to the next stop, Dunkeld and Birnam, where I would have about two and a half hours. The delay at Pitlochry station's ticket office served me well in the end because I did not see a conductor and thus saved myself a few pounds.

It being nearly five o'clock, I figured my primary mission should be to find some food. Other than that, there were only two things that Dunkeld and Birnam made me think of, and one of those was fictitious.

Hear the name of the two towns the station serves, and like me you'll maybe know that Dunkeld is famous for an old cathedral, while Birnam features in the William Shakespeare play Macbeth. I'd seen neither of them. And of course was only likely to see one of them in my time at the stop.

I was rather looking forward to my exploration here, because I knew little else about the two towns, meaning it was a proper voyage of discovery for me after a dose of familiarity with my last couple of stops. I didn't, for instance, know there was a huge river between the two villages, nor that there was quite such a long walk from Birnam, which sat next to the station, to Dunkeld, the further away of the two.

*

Birnam, which I explored first, was a pretty place and the smaller of the two villages, though still with grand buildings and wide streets. It was a couple of minutes' walk out of the station and down a hill along a tree-lined footpath.

In a modern building quite near where I arrived down into the village, there was a Beatrix Potter exhibition. It lay in the rather grand Beatrix Potter Garden, where interpretation boards told me that the famous children's author holidayed in and around Birnam, and the surrounding countryside inspired many of her stories.

Cynically, I concluded that making a big deal out of the fact that someone holidayed in your village was going a bit far. Potter never actually lived in Birnam, was not from there, and spent only a number of childhood holidays there. So her connection to it was slightly tenuous.

It reminded me of the ridiculous claim that the seaside town of Nairn, east of Inverness, has to the actor Charlie Chaplin. Based on the fact that he holidayed there a few times when in his eighties, there is, at the time of writing, discussion about creating a marked Charlie Chaplin pathway along the seafront, including statues of the man.

People who go on holiday to a place don't get to be claimed by their destination. Nairn should find its own famous people – though apart from its most famous resident, the actress Tilda Swinton, it is also the birthplace of the Thatcher-era politician William Whitelaw, and of James Augustus Grant, a nineteenth century explorer who was part of the expedition that discovered the true source of the Nile. Grant, surely, would be much more worthy of a statue for Nairn than an elderly actor who had a few holidays there.

It's the same with Birnam. It's much more famous for Macbeth than Beatrix Potter, and Macbeth, as well as being a Shakespeare character, did actually exist: he was an eleventh century Scots king. Yet I saw nothing about Macbeth, the man or the play, in my time in Birnam. Mind you, the play – as with much of the famous bard's work – was riddled with historical inaccuracies, and it is said that Shakespeare had never even visited the village himself.

I told myself that I had only just arrived and was nowhere near bored enough yet to resort to the Beatrix Potter exhibition. In any case, it was late afternoon and it was about to close.

I walked on through the village and passed a strange, modern looking wooden construct that looked more like a Canadian log cabin than a Scottish dwelling. Despite its small size, it was home to a post office, tearoom, general store and police station. It made me wonder whether the cramped conditions inside meant the whole place operated as one establishment.

"You'd like to report a crime? Certainly. Can I interest you in a postcard or a nice piece of cake while you're at it?"

Another curiosity I noticed on Birnam's main street was a series of doors on a terrace that ran 9, 7, 10, then 10a. I wondered what the story behind that strange sequence was.

I eventually turned around and took the relatively long walk towards Dunkeld, passing the rather grand Royal School of Dunkeld along the way. Its red and white art deco style stood out strikingly against the grey stone elsewhere in the two villages. Despite its grand name that had the air of a posh private establishment, it was in fact a local authority school.

Like Birnam, Dunkeld was pretty to the point of being aloof. It boasted lots of fifteenth century buildings, and of course the old, ruined cathedral. The core of the historic centre around the cathedral was a classic Scottish medieval old town, with low buildings and small roofs, but they were brightly coloured and well kept. The sky provided a contrast, though, the heavy clouds soon giving way to rain. At this late hour there wasn't much open to see around the old part of Dunkeld, not even the tourist information centre.

The cathedral itself was an impressive building. Effectively in two halves, the oldest part dated from the 1300s and had been destroyed, like many churches across Scotland, during the Reformation. It had, however, been reroofed and was now the parish church. The adjacent tower and nave, built in the fifteenth century, were in ruins, packed inside with scaffolding.

I entered the parish church to find it empty. It was a beautiful and brightly lit, if rather simple, affair, and there were a few panels explaining the origins of the church. The panels had a few things to say about other people, too, such as the Wolf of Badenoch, who lived in the fourteenth century and was excommunicated for dumping his wife. He subsequently went on a rampage in which he destroyed various churches across the north of Scotland, making today's melodramatic celebrity divorces seem rather tame.

The nave was closed off, according to a sign outside, because of falling masonry. It was hoped that it would reopen at some point. With luck, one day, I'd return to see it.

I headed back outside into the light rain and walked back along the quaint, quiet old street towards the main road. Even though it was just after the end of the working day, just one or two people passed by and the trundle of the occasional car on the cobbled roads disturbed the prim silence.

Back at the main road, near the bridge, I found the Royal Dunkeld Hotel, and figured that it was time for a pint and some food. I headed in and enjoyed an excellent plate of fish and chips and a refreshing pint of eighty shilling. There were just a few other folk in, and as I ate my attention flicked between my notebook and the subtitled BBC News channel on the television.

Maybe in good weather, during open hours and with more time Dunkeld might have been worth a deeper exploration. But the rain reflected my tiredness, and if I was honest with myself I was getting weary, walking seemingly endless amounts and carrying my small but heavy bag on my shoulders. I could have done a lot in a place like Dunkeld and Birnam overnight – walking, exploring the countryside, sampling all the pubs and so on. But I couldn't stay overnight everywhere, and as my experience in Kingussie had illustrated my overnight stops were not always a non-stop barrel of laughs.

So while I probably hadn't had the best of exposures to Dunkeld and Birnam, I could clearly see it was well worth going back. And that was the point: tasting places to see whether first impressions would encourage me to return.

As with my outward walk from the station, wisps of cloud clinging to tree lined hills in the near distance, I passed a sign on my way back pointing me down a path to Birnam Oak. A Shakespeare connection, I wondered, and in later research discovered this to be so. Although not believed to have been around at the time of King Macbeth's reign, the oak was the last survivor of the medieval Birnam Wood featured in the play. I could have walked down to it, but I was tired it was raining, and I frankly couldn't be bothered.

Once again: just me and an empty platform; signs of past life including bricked up doors and sparse premises converted into private offices; another station where hubbub had departed and the platforms lay still and lifeless, silently awaiting the next train.

CHAPTER 10: PERTH

It started to hail as I got on the train, though I didn't get too wet as I was under the canopy of the station. At twenty minutes, it was a comparatively lengthy journey. The conductor reached me on her walk-through and so I had to buy a ticket.

"Not nice," she said, and I assumed she was referring to the weather, rather than my appearance.

At about half past seven, I arrived at Perth station. Both the small city of Perth and its railway station were places I knew all too well. Sitting on the banks of the River Tay, Perth is pretty much the centre of mainland Scotland's transport network. It lies in the middle of an X formed by Scotland's main trunk roads and railway lines between Glasgow, Edinburgh, Aberdeen and Inverness, and so is an important interchange for both buses and trains from the Highlands, North East and the south of Scotland. It represented the end of the Highland Main Line and the beginning of a busier stretch of line towards Edinburgh. For my trip it was an important midpoint and gear change.

Trains from Inverness to Glasgow and Edinburgh all go through Perth, and sometimes, depending on the timetable, you need to change there. If you're getting off an Edinburgh train and want to go to Glasgow, or vice versa, thankfully you're normally waiting for only five or ten minutes – unless there's a delay, of course.

Connections are not so good for the line east to Dundee and then round the coast north to Aberdeen. Over the past few years work has taken me frequently to Dundee, an awkward place to get to by rail because the wait in Perth is often well over half an hour. And the station, sitting too long a walk from the centre of the city to make an expedition worth it in the time, is not a pleasant place to hang about in.

Given Perth is such a large station, and such a pivotal one to the rail network with huge numbers of people passing through or changing there each day, its facilities are extremely disappointing. The main concourse, bland in its modernity and looking like it was the result of a 1960s rebuild, is where you pass through to exit or pick up a taxi. It is home to a small ticket office, a WH Smith kiosk where you can buy overpriced snacks, and a greasy spoon café where you can buy even more overpriced snacks that might come hot. On many a morning after a ridiculously early start from Inverness on my way to Dundee, I would pop into the café to buy a bacon roll, a second breakfast at barely nine in the morning. Usually the café was miserable, full of other bleary-eyed travellers, and the food did nothing to inspire or awaken.

The bacon rolls usually consisted of two bits of undercooked bacon with stringy rind, with a miserly extra charge for ketchup. On one occasion I ordered a burger, which I should have known would be a bad move given it was one of those ones you took from the chilled display and handed over to be microwaved. It came back disgustingly cold and uncooked in the middle. When I took it back, the staff blasted it to smithereens to make sure it was cooked, and I found myself biting into something that was approaching the temperature of the surface of the sun.

Perth station's life-sapping ambience is entirely avoidable because it is an attractive place. Aside from the modern entrance, it is dominated by grand stone walls in a warm light brown, featuring columns and arches, all tastefully modernised by the needs of accessibility and branding, and a large vintage clock on platform seven where I usually hung around when avoiding the café. With a bit of work on the traveller experience, perhaps with an improvement in the catering and comfier seats or nice artwork on the further away platforms, it could be a real pleasure to spend time in and a place to rival the best Victorian-era station buildings in Britain. For now, though, it remains a truly soulless and unimaginative place: a traveller's purgatory.

It's not only scheduled changes but frequent delays that have seen me loiter longer than I'd like at Perth station. In bad weather, such as high winds, ice or flooding, the Highland Main Line is among the first lines to be closed. Journeys are therefore subject to delay, a replacement bus, or both.

On one occasion in December a few years ago, when I was travelling north from Glasgow to Inverness, the line had closed due to foul weather. Passengers who had changed in Perth were standing outside the station at about eight o'clock on a freezing cold winter's morning, and inevitably the railway refugee stereotypes began to emerge.

There was the angry impatient man who was obviously a middle manager type and declaring "this is absolutely unacceptable" to anyone who listened (nobody did). There was the hessian bag-carrying, shellsuit-wearing family who were trying to fend off the cold by chain-smoking. There was also a couple of earnest young Japanese tourists who hadn't a clue what was happening and didn't have enough English to ask, plus those who were too tired to complain and looked like they were trying to sleep standing up. Eventually we were loaded on to buses, and those going direct to Inverness were on a separate bus that still for some reason stopped at every station along the way, prolonging the journey beyond the exhaustion barrier.

Another time I was held up heading south, and was stranded at Perth station for some time. Though once we were all loaded into taxis the camaraderie set in, everyone trying to keep each other cheerful with jokes and shared food. While the solidarity in adversity is always a good testament to the human spirit, it's a shame that so many frequent delays have made it necessary.

Though mind you, if it hadn't been for the delays and the subsequent compensation vouchers, my stop-by-stop journey to Edinburgh would not have been quite so affordable.

Besides the station, I knew the city centre itself and the attractive riverside moderately well from various trips for work. I suppose Perth was the stop for which I was least bothered about seeking whether to return – because I knew the answer was yes. I didn't let the station cloud my judgement of the city, which boasted a picturesque riverside setting with some lovely parks and architecture.

Also, in two hours – or in this case an overnight stop – there was only so much I was going to be able to see. In a place as big as Perth, there was arguably too much to attempt to take in that would add anything of worth to my understanding of the city.

Exiting the station, then, I hopped into a taxi and headed to the edge of Perth where a friend was putting me up for the night. His name was Tom, and he was a retired gentleman who I knew through the world of Esperanto, the international language that we both spoke – or at least he spoke and I was currently learning. As two of the few speakers north of Scotland's Central Belt, we'd been put in touch by a mutual contact and had corresponded by email a few times. When I explained I would be passing through Perth as part of a rail journey, he offered me his spare room for the night.

We spent an enjoyable couple of hours chatting away in his living room in Esperanto – a story for another day, no doubt – Tom kindly but precisely correcting my errors.

At the end of the evening, while sorting my stuff in Tom's spare room I discovered that the mobile phone charger, which I'd bought in Kingussie, would not work. I'd left that morning with a full phone, but my rather old iPhone had worn its battery over the course of the day through things like texting Nicole or searching for bits and pieces of information on the web. But I had all the information I needed written on paper or in the timetables in my pocket, and it would do me no harm to try to do what centuries of travellers had done before me: manage without a phone.

I went to bed and slept incredibly deeply after a long, busy day that had started all that time ago in Dalwhinnie. I had done a lot of walking around Dalwhinnie, Blair Atholl, Pitlochry, Dunkeld and Birnam. I was satisfied that I was making such good progress, was seeing plenty interesting things along the way, and had now reached an approximate halfway point.

My next train was at eight o'clock in the morning, though Tom had very kindly offered to drive me to the station in his car. So we were up at about seven and had breakfast of tea and toast, and with a light frost on the roads we headed into town.

Tom insisted on coming to the platform to wave me off, which he did after I'd quickly popped into the ticket office to use a voucher for the next couple of journeys.

When we arrived at the platform, we discovered the rather upsetting sight of a medical emergency. A man was flat out on his back near my train being given first aid by someone in a high-visibility vest. Tom and I looked on, concerned, though it pretty quickly dawned on us that it was pointless and a little grim of us to be standing watching. I bade a quick farewell to Tom and boarded the train. As I did so, there was a call on the train's tannoy for anyone with first aid or medical experience to make themselves known to staff on the platform. Through the window I saw the man in the vest giving the patient sharp pushes to the heart.

Police officers soon appeared, and they were followed a couple of minutes later by an ambulance crew. The man on the ground didn't move, other than the vibrations of the further heart shocks given to him by the paramedics.

After a minute or two, the train moved about fifty yards down the line – making me feel guilty for having watched the incident. A young woman across the aisle from me was also looking to see what happened, and we got talking in quiet tones of concern. Given the train had moved down the line out of view of the situation, we couldn't help but assume the worst. Staff came through with bits of paper and asked for everyone's names and addresses to give to the police, and officers came through to speak to one or two people, but nobody near me seemed to have seen anything.

The woman was also, however, a little worried about missing a connection that would make her late for work. I was a bit put out by her thinking of such seemingly frivolous things, but then on the other hand, what was she supposed to do – sit and worry with no regard for her own plans? All possible help was being given, and so she had every right to think practically about what she was going to do now. Soon, a member of train staff came through the train and said we should get off and get on another train, which would leave about fifty minutes after our original scheduled departure.

It was all terribly sombre. The fact that the police were involved suggested that either it was some sort of crime or the poor man had died. A week or so after returning home, the incident still lodged in my mind – what had happened to the man? Was he alright? I had searched local newspapers online for any mention of an incident, but found nothing. In the end I called both the British Transport Police and Scotrail to ask if they could tell me. Despite making clear that I didn't want to know any personal details – simply whether the man had lived or died – both were unable to reveal anything.

I still wonder today. I never did hear from the police either, though I did get a voucher in the post from Scotrail apologising for the delay. Both voucher and apology were thoroughly unnecessary.

My journey continued, as of course it needed to, and Ladybank was my next stop. I was now done with Perthshire and would be moving into Fife. Another major phase of my adventure was underway.

CHAPTER 11: LADYBANK

I'd frequently mulled over Ladybank as I passed through on the train. It seemed a quiet place, surrounded by decrepit old warehouses, with rarely anyone getting on or off.

The town lay at an important railway junction, as this was where the northbound line from Edinburgh forked. The branch to the east headed to Dundee and Aberdeen; while the one to the west, the line I had been working my way south along, went to Perth and then of course Inverness. The fork in the line, visible from the northern end of the platform, plus an array of run-down and abandoned railway buildings, were the few suggestions of Ladybank's past importance.

The only alighting passenger, I was met with the spooky silence of commuterville on a weekday. The first thing I saw was a well-maintained village square, containing a garden and war memorial. According to the sign, this was the Haig Memorial Garden, named after Field marshal Douglas Haig who led British forces during the First World War.

Haig, whose family had Fife connections, was, to put it mildly, a controversial figure. Apparently, in the early years after the war, he was held in high affection by those who felt his leadership was a crucial factor in winning the war, and his funeral following his death in 1928 was a major state occasion.

Three years later the gardens I was now looking at in Ladybank were dedicated to his memory. The interpretation board included a quote from a senior soldier's tribute at the garden's dedication ceremony:

> "We were all very proud to know that he was a Scotsman and one of us: a man of Fife. During those fateful years from 1914 we, who survived, no less than those who fell and whose names you may read upon the Memorials scattered throughout the length and breadth of this great country of ours, did our best. We tried to do our duty cheerfully, and one of the things that enabled us to do so was the knowledge and belief and the faith in our Commander."

Of course, for the many people appalled at the carnage of the war, there would be revulsion at such cap-doffing sycophancy. With the conflict sparked by inept and arrogant political diplomacy throughout Europe, and then conducted through a hideous collision of nineteenth century military tactics with twentieth century military technology, it was one of the great evils of the modern age.

It felt wrong that the gardens should elevate commemoration of a military leader over any sort of reminder of the pointless horrors and tragedy of war.

I pressed on from the gardens to go on a wander around town. Being a Thursday morning it was hardly bouncing with life. In my amblings throughout the unremarkable streets of Ladybank I saw a butcher's, a fabric shop, a newsagent's, a couple of small supermarkets, a primary school, a tiny Episcopal chapel, a much larger Church of Scotland parish church, a restaurant called Spice café, signs for the golf club towards the far side of town, and not much else. Ladybank had the feel of a place that wasn't so much sleepy as dead.

It was clearly bin day: wheelie bins sat on roadsides, and the rumble and beep of the bin lorry disturbed the oppressive sense of quiet. I headed down Church Street, where a woman in a long dressing gown was putting out her rubbish and men were erecting scaffolding on a house. The parish church was handsome but had no major grounds or graveyard to explore. Its notice board was tired and contained few notices to speak of. Cats sat in windows of houses, and I wondered what interesting things they ever saw go by. Were they as unimpressed with Ladybank as I was?

Slightly out from the centre of the village was the Masonic Hall, a small but impressive structure. On the wall was a plaque dated 1936 that commemorated the fiftieth anniversary of the entry into the House of Commons of H H Asquith, who represented the town. Asquith, who was originally a Yorkshireman, went on to be Prime Minister from 1908-1916.

Completing a loop around the village, and nearly back at the station, I passed what seemed to be the only pub in town. Breakfast from half past seven, and half past nine on Saturday and Sunday, said the sign. The place was totally closed up.

Architecturally, Ladybank was a mix of old stone terraced houses, some bland, modern bungalows, and the occasional modest concrete municipal building. Other than the parish church and the Masonic hall, there was nothing aesthetically of merit about the town.

There was very little sign of life amongst the quiet streets. The grey skies and absence of people made for ghostly atmosphere. It was like Ladybank had been bypassed by reality, and I had slipped through some sort of vortex to explore it. To be kinder, it was probably just a quiet country village that had over time moved from being a major locus for the railways to being a commuter stop for Dundee or Edinburgh. It was funny to think that roughly halfway through my journey, with Edinburgh still a distant finishing line, some people would go there and back every morning. I wondered if they too would think about the places they passed through.

But even excusing the fact that people would be away working during the day, there was still an odd quietness to Ladybank; there was nothing to suggest it to be a place of life or culture at the evenings or weekends. With its decaying railway buildings and memorials to long-gone historical names, it truly seemed like a forgotten place.

Back at the station I found the usual sign outside that contained things like a map of the local area and onward travel information. On the map was marked an area on the edge of Ladybank called "The Wilderness".

It was not even ten o'clock and I wasn't due to leave until over an hour later. With nothing else to do and nowhere to go, other than going for a long walk out of town which I wasn't up for, I headed back to my platform and sat down. The station building, an old but modernised construction, was staffed, at least until 10am, and so I enquired about toilets. There were only staff facilities but the woman behind the counter gave me the key anyway and pointed me towards them, through a large cloakroom in an adjacent part of the building.

Back on the platform, the station was surprisingly crowded – a large gang of school-age girls and two quite young looking helpers were on the opposite platform. I thought it might be a school trip, even though it was the school holidays. They soon left on a southbound train.

Then the Aberdeen to Penzance train, according to the signs in its windows, passed through, stopping at the station to pick up another handful of people. I knew the Aberdeen to Penzance service was the longest passenger journey in the United Kingdom, taking pretty much the whole day. I fancied taking it sometime, just to say I'd done it. Though I wondered why the rail companies hadn't worked out a train from Wick to Penzance, just so it could be as long as the British rail network could possibly make it.

It passed ten o'clock, and the station office closed. Once I had the place to myself, I enjoyed the solitude and sense of abandonment, and I wandered around taking some photos. At the north end of the platform stood what might have been an old waiting room, long boarded up. Past the end of the platform lay one of the many scatterings of decaying old sheds, crumbling and overgrown with trees and weeds. Just beyond them the line to Perth stretched ahead and the Dundee line curved off to the right.

Because of the junction and the old buildings, there was an evocative sense of the station's past size. Indeed, I discovered in later research that the station was also the eastern terminus of the Fife and Kinross railway, a line that closed some years before Beeching. The main station building on the platform I stood on was itself certainly not as busy as it might once have been. Beside the ticket office, one unit was rented out as a studio, and though it was closed the pictures in the window indicated that flowers were a strong theme of the artist's work. It was good to see someone was attempting to bring some colour to Ladybank.

On the opposite platform, for northbound trains, the platform building was similarly accompanied by decaying structures, and the roof was falling in on one of them.

I sat down again on a bench on the platform. I was well and truly bored.

Forty minutes passed.

Two women, a man, and a dog came along. The dog was clearly with one woman, and the other woman and man spoke with what I thought were Canadian accents. The Canadian woman was saying that she needed to go to the loo. I didn't want to taunt her with my knowledge of the now closed station toilets, though their train arrived before she fulfilled what I hoped was a joking threat to go on the platform. The woman and dog saw them off and then left.

After that, there was a slow but steady stream of other people all coming to get trains. Now of course I could have got on any of the quite frequent southbound ones, but I didn't want to get to my next stop, Markinch, earlier than the train I had decided to take. Markinch was also a place I knew little about, and for all I knew it could be much like Ladybank. I decided it wouldn't be worth running the risk of spending extra time in a place that might turn out to just as boring, or worse. Conversely, where I was currently sitting was comfortable, dry and not particularly cold, and as I had been spending most of my journey so far walking, I was moderately content just to sit and stare into space.

Just after eleven o'clock, a woman on the platform walked up and asked me about trains to Perth. Well-versed in Ladybank train times having stared at the monitors all morning, I told her it would be the Inverness one, just after mine. Later she tried the waiting room door. I opened my mouth to say it shut at ten, but stopped myself. I didn't want her to enquire why on earth I'd been there since before ten o'clock in order to know that.

"How do you know they shut at ten?" I imagined she would ask.

"Because I've been here since before ten and the staff told me."

"What the devil are you doing sitting at Ladybank station for over an hour, you complete social incompetent?" she'd have been perfectly entitled to demand.

"I'm asking myself that question too," I would have confessed.

Thankfully, eventually, it was time for my train. The slow tick of time had finally delivered my escape. I got on board, itching to undertake my journey back to reality.

It was just eight minutes to Markinch.

CHAPTER 12: MARKINCH

After the dull horror of Ladybank, I arrived in Markinch with expectations so low they were virtually subterranean. In my head I always tended to lump Ladybank and Markinch stations together – two quiet, unremarkable stops in the north of Fife that were the last of the rural calling points before a more urban, coastal and tightly-packed series of stops on the Fife Circle, the commuter service that began at the subsequent stop Kirkcaldy. Ladybank had been boring: I expected much the same from Markinch.

My first trip was into the station building, a larger and more modern construction than at Ladybank, to visit the toilets. I was intrigued to discover that inside the gents' toilets was a urine colour chart, with an encouragement to readers to drink plenty water and to check the colour of their urine against the chart to see if they were dehydrated. I'd never seen anything like this before, even in a pub or doctor's surgery. It was Scotrail branded too, so clearly Scotland's national rail operator was branching into public health advice.

On first impressions, Markinch didn't exceed my expectations, because the town immediately struck me as pleasant and small but a little dull. It had effectively been subsumed into

Glenrothes, planned in the 1940s as one of Scotland's post-war new towns and which now served as the administrative centre of Fife Council. Glenrothes itself had no station, but was reachable from Markinch station via footpaths and cycle paths. On the other side of Glenrothes, and via the half of the Fife Circle I would not be seeing on my journey, was the optimistically named Glenrothes with Thornton, which was actually in the village of Thornton and nowhere particularly near Glenrothes.

The genteel feel to Markinch as I exited the station contrasted with the station building itself, a bold, modern building with a big square block on the opposite platform that contained a passenger lift. As I headed along what seemed to be like the main road, I stumbled across the entrance to a huge green space, Balbirnie Park. I hadn't expected much from the walk from the station, but a sign pointed me through high stone columns and into a vast park so I gladly went in for an explore. Balbirnie Park boasted vast swathes of beautiful and well-maintained greenery, trees and flowers. It was obviously a popular place for walkers and joggers, but was not unpleasantly busy. With a caravan park and golf course nearby, it was more of a country park than a city park and would have taken a long time to fully circumnavigate. I wandered around and eventually sat in silence at a picnic table in an attractive little clearing. There were trees, lots of birds, and the occasional dog walker passing by. I sat contentedly, resting my legs and writing up a few notes.

In time, I decided to head off to one of the landmarks visible from the train that I'd decided was key to this stage of the journey: a church that, though not very big, absolutely towered over humble Markinch from the top of a modest hill.

Following what seemed to be the historic high street to reach it, the church was an impressive place close up. Built in 1786, it looked older, and indeed its tower dated from the thirteenth century. The church's website later told me that there were records of preaching on the site as early as the sixth century. There was a reassuringly jumbled and decrepit graveyard around it.

It was an unexpected pleasure to wander around the vicinity of the church, which I discovered to be surprisingly rich with heritage, with old walled gardens and tightly packed lanes. The small but beautiful range of eighteenth and nineteenth century buildings had been designated a Conservation Area in the 1970s. There were lovely views across the town in all directions from this modest but commanding vantage point. It felt a world away from the soul-destroying couple of hours I'd spent at Ladybank, and in hindsight I wished I'd left Ladybank sooner to spend more time here.

Another Markinch landmark visible from the train that I had in mind was on the other side of the railway station: a big, bold building more reminiscent of the red brick industrial plants of northern England than of Fife. This was the remains of the enormous Haig's whisky bottling plant, and it towered over the open countryside to the south of the town. Its red, angular appearance felt a little out of place among the softer tones and edges of Markinch's historic buildings. But it was certainly not ugly, and it boasted a commanding position facing southwards across the valley and the railway viaduct to its left, over which I would soon cross on my next leg. Whenever I would head north on the train, the white letters "John Haig & Co Ltd, Markinch" on its facing wall would stand out from some distance.

No longer used for its original purpose, the site was now seemingly divided into individual industrial and commercial units. One was a car repair garage, other parts offices. Not all of it was in use, so the buildings had more than a few boarded up windows, and weeds grew around about. There was also a railway siding, suggesting that a train track had, once upon a time, branched off to serve the bottling factory. From certain angles through the wire fence, the place had an aura of a long-abandoned prison.

Heading down a path, the old factory on my right and the line stretching ahead on the left over the viaduct, I passed two older men chatting. A few minutes later after taking in the view, I decided to turn back. I stopped nearby them to photograph the Haig building again.

"You're not taking photos of us too?" one of the men said, in a light-hearted, mock indignation.

The quip rather caught me on the hop and I couldn't get my brain in gear to think of a witty response – though with inevitable afterthought I devised a cheeky retort about photographing the decrepit old relics of Markinch. In that split second, though, I just chuckled and stumbled out a "hello" to the boisterous spaniel that one of them had on a leash, and who was leaping up and straining to greet me. The men must have thought I was a bit of a simpleton unused to meeting people.

But it dawned on me some moments later that they were among the very few people outside customer service roles I'd spoken to that day, or indeed on the entire trip.

I thought back over my trip so far about the "real" human interaction I'd had. I couldn't think of many. I'd been travelling alone, after all. The occasional pleasantry with people on trains sprang to mind, including the unstoppably chatty woman on my very first train to Carrbridge, but that was about it.

I'd not exactly been digging deep in the towns I was visiting, nor having probing conversations with locals - but then, why would I or should I have had such experiences? I certainly wasn't expecting to randomly bump into local history experts at each stop, and a stranger can't expect to be accosted by friendly locals all the time. This wasn't some romantic, fictionalised view of Scotland where the red carpet is cheerily rolled out for me as I breeze into each new place. It was very real, very everyday and frankly very ordinary Scotland.

A big part of the reason was that I didn't particularly stand out. My journey was not being undertaken as an eye-catching gimmick, so there was nothing about my appearance or behaviour to make people notice or speak to me. Nor did I have an unusual or foreign accent, often a dependable conversation starter. While this anonymity served me well, allowing me to observe and explore without attracting unwanted attention, it also cut me off from much in the way of revealing conversations with locals. I was surprised at how few people I'd spoken to, in retrospect, but it had never been a particular part of my plan.

Back at Markinch station, I was in good time for my train to Kirkcaldy. It had been a pleasant couple of hours, with the park, the old town round the church and the proud decay of the old Haig's plant giving me a much-needed lift of the spirits after Ladybank. I could easily have spent more time here. And I would not have objected to visiting again some day.

CHAPTER 13: KIRKCALDY

The nine-minute journey to Kirkcaldy was a major change of pace for my adventure. So far, my journey was along a main branch line between Inverness and Edinburgh, and not every train going along it would stop at every single station. That meant that while the Inverness to Edinburgh services tended to be a couple of hours apart, my wait had tended be much longer at the smaller stations as not every train stopped there.

That created a challenge for my planning to make sure I visited the wee places for their full, allotted times. They were also, of course, often a long way from each other, as evidenced by the journeys of over fifteen minutes between, for instance, Inverness and Carrbridge, Dalwhinnie and Blair Atholl, or Dunkeld and Perth, journeys in which I could actually relax for a wee while.

However, Kirkcaldy was not just served by the line from Inverness and Perth to Edinburgh, but by the Fife Circle too. From Kirkcaldy there were therefore two directions I could take on the circle. In one direction, the line headed west and inland, through the likes of Dunfermline and Cowdenbeath, while in the other direction it hugged the coast for five stops, including Kirkcaldy itself, before the loop met again at Inverkeithing and headed south over the Forth Bridge towards

Edinburgh. This was the route I would be taking, overlapping as it did with the line from Perth.

In a sense the Fife Circle was the bit that held most mystery to me. Because it was principally a commuter route, the Inverness to Edinburgh train would never stop anywhere on the Fife Circle other than Kirkcaldy and occasionally Inverkeithing. Instead it would tend to shoot along the coast through all these little coastal towns and villages which I mostly knew very little about and which, because of the steep cliffs and the distractions of the lovely views of the Firth of Forth, weren't easy to see in any detail.

Being a commuter service, the Fife Circle stops were close together. Most were just a couple of minutes apart and trains ran several times an hour – or, at worst, every half hour at quiet times. Therefore, planning this part of the journey had been easy. I could stick to my rough minimum of two hours or so in each place, and then head to the station knowing that there would not be long to wait until the next train.

Kirkcaldy, the biggest place I would visit between Perth and Edinburgh, always made me think of that famous Madonna hit "Erotic". The song contained the racy lyrics "erotic, erotic, run your hands all over my body", which was well known for being misheard as "Bill Oddie, Bill Oddie, run your hands all over my body" – a mental image I think we could all do without. However, when I passed through the station, I always thought of the line "Kirkcaldy, Kirkcaldy, run your hands all over my body." Not that I'm much into Madonna, of course. Or Bill Oddie, for that matter.

More seriously, there were two other things I always noticed when I passed Kirkcaldy, and in the absence of much knowledge about the town, I figured they should be the main anchors for my time there.

One was a seemingly huge sprawl of abandoned and decaying factories at the northern end of the town. They heralded the train's arrival in the town (from the north, anyway), giving the unsuspecting visitor that they were approaching some sort of post-apocalyptic wilderness. Some in ruins, some covered in graffiti, and many sitting quite surprisingly close to the bustle of the rest of town, they presented an enticing opportunity for exploration.

The second thing I had in mind was the Raith Rovers Football Club stadium, Stark's Park, at the other end of town. Sitting very close to the line, so close in fact you could see the pitch between the stands as you went by on the train, it was pretty much the first landmark you would see in Kirkcaldy if approaching from the south. Fans of rival teams are welcome to insert their own jokes here about Stark's Park being a similarly abandoned wasteland to the crumbling factories.

My first discovery in Kirkcaldy was the seafront. It took me rather by surprise, and I realised it was quite a milestone for my journey. On my fourth day I'd made it right across the middle of Scotland and arrived once more at the sea – from the Moray Firth to the Firth of Forth. I knew of course that the train headed towards the coast from Markinch, and that you could see the Firth of Forth over the houses from the railway line beyond that, but I had no idea that Kirkcaldy, although on the coast, had such a big harbour and such a lovely long beach. It rather shifted my perception of the place – no longer was it just about the old industries in the once-intact factories, but also the industries of the sea.

Kirkcaldy contained some nice old buildings, too – such as a historic customs house and a lovely art deco fire station. There were also more than a few nice churches, with some pretty parts of town nestled around the harbour. The scale of the civic buildings and the size of this historic royal burgh was a refreshing change. After Ladybank and Markinch it was nice to be somewhere where there was a bit of a buzz.

The town also boasted a few busy shopping streets, and as I headed down to the seafront I saw a Gregg's bakery. It was lunchtime so I bought a pie and a delicious caramel fudge doughnut. As there was no Gregg's in Inverness, I rarely visited the otherwise ubiquitous bakery chain, so it was a pleasing novelty. Well, they say travel broadens the mind and opens you up to new experiences.

With little to base my impressions on except the ruined factories and Raith Rovers' stadium, Kirkcaldy was a much more attractive town than I had expected. I sat at the seafront and ate my lunch, and though it was a fairly cold day it was still sunny and I felt refreshed by the crisp sea air. A few folk were walking along the promenade or, like me, sitting and taking in the view. To the left of the seafront as I looked out to sea were a mix of decaying old harbour buildings and smart looking flats, while the high street was to my right.

Moving on, I switched inland and followed what seemed to be an arterial road through the town running northeast, behind which lay the railway line, and I soon arrived at the abandoned old factories I'd had my eye on. They were an impressive array of rusting corrugated iron structures and some stone buildings with one or two quite ornate features that belied their decaying state. Lying empty and perhaps awaiting redevelopment, they stood as a testament to the town's history in textiles and linoleum, which were major industries in the nineteenth century.

It was of course different now – the industry long gone, the buildings fenced off, boarded up and covered in warning signs outside to keep people out. I was sure they attracted urban explorers at night. Yet another long lost aspect of Scotland's industrial history, the shells that once contained hundreds of workers now all lay dormant along the road I was now following. Cars and the occasional pedestrian passed by, maybe oblivious to the history they were passing.

I soon tired, walking as I was at quite a pace. The density of buildings began to thin as I headed towards the edge of town, with fewer interesting old buildings to see. I could see trains pass occasionally, helping me to contextualise the large, blockish old factories that I would first see when heading south towards Edinburgh. But conscious that I had to keep to time and that I also wanted to take in the football stadium, I turned around and headed back.

*

On my way back through the centre of town, I came across a sign on a stretch of open grass, a modest plaque on a pole commemorating "Sir Sandford Fleming, 1827-1915", a son of Kirkcaldy who had emigrated to Canada. There, the text informed me, he had invented standard time (as you do) and was chief engineer of the Canadian Pacific Railway. He was clearly a man of some eminence and achievement in his adopted land, and the plaque was erected, so it said, by the Archaeological and Historical Sites Board of the Ontario government. I found a photo online later of an identical plaque, erected in a park named after him in Peterborough, Ontario.

How typical, I thought, that it was the Canadians not we Scots who made a big deal of him. It seemed so often that people had to leave Scotland to be recognised. He was clearly famous there, yet I'd never heard of him, and I suspected many folk in Kirkcaldy hadn't either.

Fleming wasn't the only famous person from Kirkcaldy to be immortalised in a plaque, however. Elsewhere in the town I noticed a modest plaque in the ground in a small park. It was a small circle no more than a thirty centimetres or so in diameter, and was erected by Kirkcaldy Civic Society. It read:

"Author, poet and diarist Marjory Fleming 'Pet Marjorie' was buried here in 1811, aged 8 years 11 months."

She was seemingly was the daughter of an accountant in the town, and kept a diary for the last year and a half of her life before dying young. It was obviously a sad tale, though touching that she had been memorialised in this way.

After a seemingly endless trek in the sunshine through streets of monotonous stone terraced houses, I arrived at the football stadium at the other end of the town. Though a long walk, there had been no risk of getting lost. I knew, after all, that the stadium was right next to the railway so it was just a case of following the road as close to the line as I could.

Raith Rovers, who as I write are in Scottish football's second tier, have had flashes of fame and success in what is an otherwise predictably unremarkable history for a provincial club. Their biggest achievement in the modern era was arguably when they beat Celtic in the final of the 1994 League Cup. It was a shock not only because they had beaten one of the two giants of Scottish football, but also because at the time they were still in the second tier. As a result of their cup win they became the first Scottish team from outside the top flight to qualify for European competition, although in the same year they also won their division and were promoted for the following season.

In the next year's European adventure, Raith Rovers beat Faroese and Icelandic teams in the early rounds of the UEFA Cup, then came up against the mighty Bayern Munich. They lost 2-0 at home in the first leg, in a match relocated to Edinburgh because their stadium was not fit for such a big game. But in the second leg, they astonishingly led at half-time in Munich's famous Olympic Stadium before eventually losing 2-1 on the night and 4-1 on aggregate. Apparently when Stark's Park was redeveloped as an all-seater stadium, Bayern Munich were invited to its first game for a friendly, and Raith Rovers won 1-0.

I distinctly remember all the joyous headlines at their great success around that time, not least one after winning the cup that read "Raith dance into Europe", an allusion to a legendary broadcasting error made in the 1960s. Following a reported win for the club, a television reporter said there would be "dancing in the streets of Raith" that evening. But there was, of course, no such town as Raith, the club taking their name from a historic estate in the area rather than the name of the home town. The error, as much as the club's entry into Europe, has given Raith Rovers a special little place in Scottish football folklore.

As if that wasn't enough exciting history for one club, Raith

Rovers are also surely one of the only football clubs in the world to have been shipwrecked. Back in 1922, the club went to the Canary Islands to play some friendly matches after a particularly successful season. However, their ship hit rocks on the coast of Spain. Although everyone was evacuated safely and the team completed its tour successfully, it was still a dramatic and unusual chapter of football history.

But when I took in the spectre of Stark's Park, I discovered it to be just a football stadium: modern, bland and unremarkable. Not that I had any reason to find anything else.

After the long walk, I was absolutely done in. I turned around and walked all the way back to the station.

Arriving exhausted and sweating, I had half an hour or so until my intended departure time, so I stripped off my fleece to put in my bag, and sat on a bench on the platform. I rested my aching feet and allowed myself to cool down somewhat despite the sun remaining enjoyably bright.

Bizarrely, two young backpackers got off a train from the south, and began asking questions of a woman on the platform, though I could not hear what about. Pleasant though Kirkcaldy was, I didn't think it was especially interesting to tourists – except for fans of abandoned old factories and provincial town football stadiums.

Mind you, I was a kind of tourist. And what on earth was I doing in Kirkcaldy? I was shattered by the end of my time there, so I was beginning to wonder what I was letting myself in for in this adventure. I hadn't realised quite what a long hike it would be to the ruined factories, back through town, onwards to the football stadium and back once more to the station. Only later did I discover that Kirkcaldy's nickname was The Lang Toon.

If only I'd known.

CHAPTER 14: KINGHORN

Four o'clock: another train, this time to Kinghorn. I knew very little about this destination, though was aware from previous journeys that the town was rather hidden away, seemingly clinging to a cliff and overlooking the Firth of Forth.

Drawn by past glimpses of the sand at the bottom of the incline on which Kinghorn precariously sat, I headed from the station down a steep path to find a lovely beach, harbour and church, tucked away from the bulk of the rest of the town.

It was warm though not fully summery, and families were playing on the sand and sitting outside a little ice cream shop. I bought an ice cream and sat on the beach while the laughs and shouts of toddlers competed with the squawks of seagulls. It was as if I'd accidentally stumbled on to the English seaside.

The buildings facing across the beach and out to sea included a lifeboat station and hotel, the latter somewhat missing a trick by lacking a beer garden, given its ideal location for customers to sit and drink a refreshing pint in the sunshine. Behind the buildings lay tightly packed houses and narrow lanes – typical for what I supposed was historically a fishing community.

The view out to sea was across the firth to Edinburgh, a glimpse of my final destination. The coastline opposite stretched out eastwards towards North Berwick, and I could also see what a later check of a map confirmed to be Inchkeith, one of the few islands in the firth. Inchkeith is home today to just a lighthouse (and birds, obviously), but housed military fortifications at various points in history as well as being an occasional location for exiled plague sufferers.

Perhaps Inchkeith's oddest chapter was an experiment conducted by King James IV in 1493, when he sent a mute woman to the island along with two babies. His macabre idea was for the woman to rear the children without the ability to teach them to talk, in order to discover what language they would acquire. The king assumed that they would grow up speaking the original language of God. Needless to say, his hypothesis was not borne out.

The little church at the end of the beach, sitting close to a finger of land that jutted a little out into the sea, was Kinghorn Parish Church. The closed gates leading to the churchyard had no less than five signs on it. One warned me that they had "forensic systems" in place to protect against metal theft. Two others told me to keep dogs on leads and not let them foul. One from Fife Council Bereavement Services told me to beware of unstable headstones, and the last one told me that work in the churchyard had been done by offenders through the community service scheme. Enticed by this comprehensively warm welcome I went in, my head turning as a train zipped across the viaduct high up behind me.

The church building itself struck me as rather peculiar. You got a good view of it from the train as you rushed past, but it always seemed out of place against the rest of Kinghorn. A plain structure with a high-angled roof, it had a square tower that was topped by two tall arches on each side. If it were a bit more of a sun-blasted colour, it would not have looked out of place somewhere in southern Europe.

The graveyard was clearly old, scattered with various monuments and headstones, precarious and weathered just as the sign had warned. Round the back of the church, next to an wall that was crumbling and overgrown, lay some much older headstones, words long faded and now hard to read. Over the low wall of the churchyard was a view back down towards the beach I'd just been sitting at. It was a serene setting and I appreciated a brief chance to chill out after all the walking in Kirkcaldy.

In one part of the churchyard sat a large stone cairn, clearly a modern addition, with a plaque on it that read:

"Kinghorn Parish Church
To celebrate
The third millennium A.D.
Jesus Christ
The same yesterday, today,
And forever."

I thought celebrating the third millennium was a bit premature given we were only about one percent of the way through it. Perhaps they ought to have waited a few centuries to be sure that it was not going to turn into one of those disappointingly bloody and war-filled millenniums like the one we've just finished.

After the churchyard I headed back up the road that led under the railway viaduct. The railway line essentially split the town between what felt like a cute, if decaying, old fishing village, and a slightly less cute but equally decaying upper town. I passed a small bit of landscaped ground that, according to a sign, had been worked on by more community payback scheme offenders. Either there was lots of work to do in Kinghorn, or lots of offenders. Perhaps both.

I passed more tired old buildings, some abandoned, boarded up and crumbling, and another with scaffolding, plus a few monstrosities from the 1970s. I walked along the main street where there were a few more attractive buildings amongst the air of decrepitude.

Given that it was approaching five o'clock in the afternoon, and given I'd spent a long afternoon walking, I figured it was time for a beer and a nice sit down. Apart from an abandoned looking motel I could find just one pub in town, sitting halfway along the main street. According to the sign its name was the Crown Tavern. From the outside it looked dark and had frosted windows, and had an unwelcoming, locals-only feel. I never trust pubs that you can't see into from outside, especially when you're alone and in a strange place. But it was the only ostensible option.

I have a bad feeling about this, I told myself. Fearing a gritty boozer of the worst kind, I pushed the narrow doors and stepped into the gloom.

"I'm sure C S Lewis was born in St John's Wood," a man at the bar was loudly insisting. I'm not sure what I was expecting to find inside the Crown Tavern, but a heated debate about the birthplace of the eminent Christian writer and author of the Chronicles of Narnia was not among my top guesses. And sadly for the group huddled around the bar, Belfast wasn't among their top guesses, which I discovered later was the answer to their question.

Nobody particularly turned as I came in, though there was a pleasant and amiable vibe from the clientele, perhaps about ten or so all in late middle age or older. I went to the bar and ordered a pint of Best from the smiling barmaid, and sat at a table near the door.

"I'm never playing whist on a Thursday with Fran Turner again," someone at the bar was complaining. "She always wins." That day was Thursday, so they must have started whist early if it was that week they were talking about.

There was a pool table further back into the bar, but nobody was playing. The tables around the pub were mostly empty, the customers tending to gravitate around the bar. On the other side of the door from me, to my right, was a coat stand, with someone's shopping and a bag of loo roll at its feet. The day's newspapers sat in a rack on the wall to my left, so I grabbed one and began reading. I wasn't really paying attention to it – it was more a case of displacement activity as my phone battery was nearly dead and I'd turned it off earlier.

Enjoying the chance to relax and take the weight off my

aching feet, I finished my paper and my pint at a leisurely place but without anyone talking to me, and I ambled down to the station for about half past six.

It was just me and three teenaged boys, two of them with bikes, on the quiet and empty platform. The train, when it arrived, was something of a relic. Rather than the usual Scotrail livery, the carriages were a dark red and had old-fashioned turn handle doors and old British Rail notices on the walls inside. Perhaps they had been short of stock that day and were having raid museums to fulfil services.

I didn't have time to dwell on the matter, though, or indeed on my time in Kinghorn, as it was only a couple of minutes until my next stop.

CHAPTER 15: BURNTISLAND

Burntisland was, thankfully, the last stop of the day. It was fortuitous that my schedule included an overnight stop there, as I had a friend in the town with whom I'd arranged to stay. As I couldn't use the map on my now-dead phone, I checked his address – which thankfully I had written down in my notebook earlier – against the map at the station. I found it easily and headed on my way.

Alan was an old friend from university, and had lived in Burntisland for some years. Though I'd of course passed through the town many times, I had never stopped there and had never visited him, until now.

After finding his house, and having a chance to dump my bag and get a cup of tea, Alan suggested we went for a walk around town while it was still light.

Burntisland was an interesting place to observe as you passed on the train – if you weren't looking out to sea. Part of it was reminiscent of the New Town in Edinburgh, prim and proper and neat with a towering church, and a long green park between the grand houses and the railway line. Once you went under the line by way of a short tunnel, you reached the seafront and beach, though there was not much to see of it today, perhaps because the tide was in.

On my regular journeys south I would see the beach, which at low tide was a beautiful sight, the morning sunlight scattering a glistening sheen across the sand, broken only by the occasional dog walker. Beyond the sands lay the firth, and then, in the distance, Edinburgh.

Another part of Burntisland, however, was centred on the shipyards that the town was known for – sprawling industrial complexes of mangled metal, cranes and noise further along the seafront. Burntisland's heavy industry was long past its heyday, but some still remained.

Alan and I did a circle through the town taking in all the key sights. We went through the grand Victorian streets, across the park and under the railway line. I could see Inchkeith, now further over to my left, a welcome indicator of some progress on my journey. To my left the beach stretched round and then there was a headland, beyond which lay Kinghorn. To the right, there was a promontory past which sat a curious jumble of old houses and a very modern sports centre.

We headed in that direction, towards the shipyard, following a rough pathway and passing an old church high on the promontory where Alan pointed out steps leading up from the sea, allowing fishermen to reach the church directly. Signs for the Fife Coastal Path reminded me that there was an alternative mode of transport for my route, at least along this stretch. Suddenly, out of nowhere, the path turned into a tarmac double track road, complete with white road markings, which led us to industrial sheds and other constructions that heralded our move into the shipyards and harbour. We were soon joined by a long-abandoned railway line, another sign of the scale that industry had once been in the past.

The views out to sea showed that Edinburgh was edging closer. I could see more detail, such as Leith, Arthur's Seat and the Pentland hills beyond.

We turned right inland again, cranes towering over us, past some old buildings including what was once a customs house. There was a street imaginatively named Harbour Place, and a railway bridge over the road.

Things widened out into grander, taller buildings of what would have perhaps been the main commercial hub. There was a plaque highlighting the royal connections of the town, including James V, who had developed the harbour and granted status of Royal Burgh to Burntisland; Mary Queen of Scots, who had been a frequent visitor; and Charles I, who had "lost his potentially priceless treasure when his baggage ferry sank off Burntisland in 1633." There was even mention of Cromwell, whose forces occupied the town for nine years, "subjecting the inhabitants to a period of great tyranny and oppression."

Another interpretation further on revealed a few facts about the town, including how it was home to the earliest still-used post-reformation churches, as well as one of the two stopping points for the world's first roll-on roll-off ferry (the other end being Granton, to the north of Edinburgh). Visible through some trees from the harbour was Rossend Castle, built in 1119 by abbots from Dunfermline, but now privately owned.

As we walked, Alan was interested to hear more about my journey so far. Like me he travelled a great deal for his work, though tended to drive rather than take the train.

"I remember once, though," he said, "being on the train and overhearing someone ask the conductor for a ticket to Marrakech. It took me a minute to realise he'd said 'Markinch'." An easy mistake but an important distinction, given that Morocco had yet to be incorporated into the Fife circle – and this remains the case at the time of writing.

Burntisland wasn't just about the coast. Thanks to the town's growth as a commuter town for Edinburgh, housing had spread inland in recent decades. The town, appropriately enough, reminded me of the sea – waves of modest hillsides, covered in low density housing, ebbing and flowing away from the coast, hidden from the view of those on the train, and reaching a pinnacle with The Binn, a hill that Alan said was only thirty minutes' climb. Also in that direction lay the home of Burntisland Shipyard FC, another of the few things I had known about the town, thanks to the lower league team occasionally cropping up in the early rounds of the Scottish Cup. Though we didn't pass the ground on our walk, I did hear cheering, shouting and a football whistle when I first got off the train at Burntisland, so could place the rough direction of it.

Much of the town's newer housing, Alan explained, was built on the site of old aluminium works, another of the town's past industries. Along with the shipbuilding, it had been a major employer.

Alan himself had grown up in the Borders and remembered holidaying in Burntisland. "The fair still comes through the summer," he explained. "I remember once as a child winning one of the fairground games and the prize was an ashtray."

Times have thankfully changed somewhat.

After returning to the house, we chatted over a delicious dinner and into the evening. I called Nicole on Alan's phone. He didn't have a charger that fitted my phone, and I didn't know when I would next have a chance to speak to Nicole. On the one hand, it was a strangely outmoded conversation, having to make plans for her to meet me once my journey was over and to let her know my progress in a way I couldn't continually do by text or quick mobile calls each evening. On the other hand, it made the journey seem more adventurous, like I was all the further from home.

At the end of a busy day of seemingly endless walking, I slept terrifically well. It was with some trepidation that I cast my mind ahead to the following day, however, as it would be another full one. I would only be going the short distance to South Queensferry, but that would involve five train journeys and five new places to discover along the way.

CHAPTER 16: ABERDOUR

I headed off just after nine o'clock on the Thursday morning, the fifth and penultimate day of my journey.

I knew exactly what I wanted to focus on when I got to my first destination of the day, Aberdour. In amongst other glimpsed scenes like holiday caravans, church spires, houses and of course abandoned factories to see on this particular stretch of the line, there was a rather curious and out of place structure: Aberdour Castle.

Sitting on my frequent train journeys, the castle always slightly took me by surprise, sitting as it did right in the town and immediately adjacent to the railway line. It stood out as a peculiar remnant against the backdrop of the world round about it: a sizeable ruin encroached upon by the sands of modernity. Knowing little else about Aberdour, the castle seemed a natural first port of call. It was a short walk from the station.

The first sign I passed pointing me to the castle boasted that one could "visit the home of the most powerful man in Scotland". Whether that was Alex Salmond or Donald Trump, the sign was unclear.

At only a five pounds entry fee, according to the sign, I

reasoned it was worth paying. Yet despite it being just after half past nine the ticket office and shop were not open. I would have paid but couldn't, so I explored the ruins and the impressive gardens by myself.

There was not much in the way of signs or interpretations to tell me about the castle as I walked round it, though having not bought a ticket I presumably was missing out on some extra background information – not least who Scotland's most powerful man was. It was a bright and dry morning, so I enjoyed the chance to amble around in the sunshine.

The castle was fairly modest in size, and in the typical medieval style – quite functional rather than aesthetically eye-catching, but with some more modern additions too. Built around the year 1200, I discovered later, and therefore one of the two oldest surviving castles in Scotland, Aberdour was frequently extended over the years. However it was abandoned from the early 1700s, with a fire and a couple of collapsed walls leaving the place in some considerable ruin. Fallen parts of the castle still lay where they had landed over the centuries.

The castle's large doocot, the neatly terraced lawns and the ornately crafted stonework of the walls all had a weathered feel about them. They made for sharp black and white photos against the bright blue sky.

I perhaps should have waited for the office to open so I could do a more thorough visit, but at least I knew it would be a place worthy of a return one day.

On my way out, exiting through a stone archway, I saw an old house, with a name plaque that read "Dour Cottage". Of course this was a hint to the town's name, with "dour" being an archaic Gaelic word for water, but I couldn't help wondering if it wasn't the best advert for the personalities of its occupants.

I headed along what seemed to be the main road through the town, lined with attractive houses and the usual small businesses, and saw a sign for Shore Street. Guessing correctly what might be at the end of it (I ought to be a detective, you know), I headed down the steep road.

Black Sands, a sign told me when I reached the bottom of the road; though the sand was anything but black. Thanks to the clear weather, I was greeted with another view across the forth, and again my landscape was changing, clear evidence of my painfully gradual movement along the coast. From left to right, I saw what I assumed was Tranent power station, the sands of Musselburgh, the towers of Leith, Arthur's Seat, Edinburgh's Old Town and castle, and another island in the firth, Inchcomb Island, with the outline of buildings on it visible against the horizon.

Inchcomb Island was notable for being the home of an ancient former abbey, and was named after St Columba who supposedly visited. It was possible to reach it by way of a boat from South Queensferry.

It was both encouraging and frustrating to see my final destination across the water. It seemed so close, yet I wouldn't be there until the next afternoon and there were plenty stops still to come.

I sat on a bench at the sands, resting, water lapping on the shore. A few dog walkers passed. There was sunshine, a slight smell of seaweed, and the gentlest of breezes. My legs and feet were crying out for more rest, but I'd not seen the entire centre of the village and had another hour to go according to my schedule. So I picked myself up again, swung my bag on to my back, and trudged on once more.

Walking along the road and past a bridge over the railway line, I saw a small open space with seating. It was, according to the sign, an "Old School Sensory Garden". Presumably this meant it was a sensory garden based in an old school, rather than one where hipsters would hang out and insist that the newer sensory garden down the road just wasn't as good. Seemingly intending to appeal to all senses and engage visually impaired visitors, there were a few signs with Braille translations that explained a little about the sights, sounds and smells of the garden – from fragrant flowers to wind chimes and bird feeders that drew in chirps and tweets.

One board, curiously not translated into Braille, said that the site held the original Aberdour Primary School and headmaster's house, built in 1850. The first head to occupy it lived during the age of the steam train, and due to the proximity of the railway line family meals had to be timed between trains as the crockery bounced around from the vibrations.

I headed out of the garden.

"Simon!"

Squinting into the low morning sun, I could vaguely see a couple of women across the road, one waving at me.

This was somewhat unusual.

Unable to see through the bright glare, I cross the road and into the shade, and discovered it was a former colleague of mine from Inverness, Marie.

"What on earth are you doing here?" we asked each other. She was down visiting a friend overnight. The friend was with her and we were introduced. We had a good catch up – it had been some years since we'd last spoken – and I told her all about my journey. It was a delightful small-world moment, and it was refreshing to talk to some real people for a bit. In time, they and I headed off again in our respective directions and I was left once more in my own little world and to my own little adventures.

Further on past the sensory garden on the edge of the village was a cemetery. A modest stone archway bridged the entrance, and there was graffiti at the top of the arch that read "No surrender". Disappointingly, they'd not written "surrender" on the other side.

After an walk through the cemetery, which was pleasant but unremarkable, I judged I'd seen pretty much all the major highlights of Aberdour over the past couple of hours. Tired, I headed back to the station, following a path that had been done up courtesy of Fife Council's ubiquitous community payback scheme.

Aberdour was a pretty place, I concluded, though small and sleepy. Perhaps it would be nice to return to for a wee visit one day if I was in the area. And if the castle office was open.

CHAPTER 17: DALGETY BAY

If Aberdour, with its attractive shoreline, ancient castle and lovely old buildings, had been a pleasant place to hang out, my first impression of Dalgety Bay was that it would be the complete opposite.

I got off the train at a quiet, unmanned station to be greeted by a dual carriageway, beyond which the town seemed to lie: a disheartening sprawl of suburbia plus low-density commercial units including a supermarket, garden centre and car showroom. Dalgety Bay was clearly a bland, dull commuter town, a world away from the quaintness of Aberdour or the muscular industrial grandeur of Burntisland.

I studied the map at the station, wondering how on earth I could fill my time on a late weekday morning in Dalgety Bay, a town I knew absolutely nothing about. The map showed a circular walk, which cut through the town and joined the Fife Coastal Path for a spell before looping back round again to the station. With nothing else evident to do, I took a photo of the map for reference and headed off.

My journey began with a trudge through a large swathe of the town, including seemingly countless roundabouts and semi-detached houses with posh cars outside. All very well to do; all very boring.

Following a sign down a little footpath at the end of an otherwise unassuming cul de sac, I went through unkempt scrubland and a small wood, and then arrived at the shore. The stony beach was fenced off with a flimsy wooden fence and there were signs posted along it:

"PUBLIC NOTICE – DALGETY BAY

RADIOACTIVE CONTAMINATION

Radioactive contamination has been found on this beach. This may pose a risk to public health through skin contact or inadvertent swallowing of contaminated items."

The sign, erected by SEPA, the environment agency, went on to say that people should keep off and that a monitoring and recovery programme was in place. I could see a couple of folk on the beach dressed head to foot in the sort of protective covers you see crime scene investigators wearing in police dramas, walking slowly around and taking samples from the ground to put into buckets.

This rang a bell from the news, now I thought about it. I could vaguely recall reports in the past few months about the radioactive finds, and how the beach had been closed off. Though with Dalgety Bay hardly being on my radar, I hadn't taken in the precise details. Alarmingly, I read later on SEPA's website that radioactive items had been found as early as 1990. According to various sources, the radioactive material had been dumped around fifty years ago, and the local Member of Parliament, former prime minister Gordon Brown, had blamed the Ministry of Defence. However, no guilt appears to have been admitted by any party, and the risks have been deemed low.

Moving swiftly on, I passed a sailing club, the yard filled with rows of small boats and one or two people cleaning or painting them.

Then I got my first views of the Forth bridges: the three red humps of the rail bridge standing bold against the sky and sea, and the grey pillars of the road bridge visible beyond. It was an important marker in my journey along the Fife coast, and I would reach the bridges later that afternoon.

I walked on, passing some grand houses with lovely views of the firth. Checking my watch and realising that I didn't want to be here all day, and aware of my schedule and my tiredness, I cut back inland. I was glad I did, because as I followed a different footpath I stumbled across an old chapel, sitting roofless, abandoned and overgrown inside, with pigeons flying in and out. It was a stark and odd contrast to the prim, tree-lined suburbia around about, almost like a portal into a past time, a piece of forgotten history that someone had forgotten to erase.

Later research led me to discover that this was Donibristle chapel, a mortuary built in the eighteenth century for the Earls of Moray. The surrounding estate land had obviously all since been built upon, leaving the chapel standing alone and anomalous in the middle of trees. It was an engagingly spooky surprise.

In looking into Donibristle chapel after my trip, I also stumbled across references to St Bridget's church, a ruin on the outskirts of Dalgety Bay. It was consecrated in 1244 but there was mention of a church on the site in a papal document of the previous century. I had seen no sign for St Bridget's church in my time in the town. It was an testament to what can lie hidden away out of sight, in amongst the most ordinary and inauspicious surroundings.

By the time I returned to the station, taking a long walk through more blandness, it was only an hour and a half since I first arrived at the stop. This was less than my stipulated two-hour minimum, but I really couldn't be bothered spending any more time in Dalgety Bay. In any case, a radioactive beach and abandoned old chapel were infinitely more than I would have expected to find when I first stepped on to that empty station platform.

CHAPTER 18: INVERKEITHING

It was just three minutes to Inverkeithing, a journey not even worth sitting down for. It was something of a refreshing change getting off in what felt to be a larger place than any anywhere I'd been since Kirkcaldy.

Unlike the other stops along the Fife coast, I had some connection to Inverkeithing: I had lived there for three years. Admittedly it was when I was very small, before I went to school. I had been born in Dingwall and lived the first year of my life in Invergordon, but my dad had left his job in local government to train for the Church of Scotland ministry, so we lived in Inverkeithing for three years while he commuted each day to Edinburgh to study.

Of course, I didn't really remember much about the place – not only was it a long time ago but inevitably memories can get clouded and confused with other early phases of life. So it wasn't as if there were floods of emotions and long-forgotten memories rushing back to me when I got off the train.

For something to focus on while exploring Inverkeithing, I set myself the challenge of finding our old house. While I didn't remember our address – and my phone of course was dead so I couldn't phone my parents to check – I did recall one important detail: it was directly over the railway line.

I vaguely remember the big garden at the back of the house and seeing trains rush underneath and into the tunnel, but don't remember – probably for the best – the earth-shattering noise my parents tell me that trains made as they trundled beneath the house at all hours of day and night.

Armed with that bare information, I headed off on my little detective hunt. Scouting out my surroundings to find where the tunnel was, I walked right round a car park next to the station and over an abandoned single rail line, and that allowed me to see where the main line went into a tunnel. A house sat directly above it. Location identified, I looped back round and headed up the hill to where the front of the house would be.

It was smaller than I remember. Had I not been somewhat less self-conscious I might have got down on my hands and knees, to toddler level, to see if that gave me a more evocative perspective. I looked at the street name, which did ring a bell, as did the façade of the house and the big wooden gates that my dad had to keep painting over to cover up graffiti.

This area, and the town generally, had a slightly rough, lost feel about it. Across the road there was a Christmas shop. Either it was shut down, or it was doing a less than roaring trade during this Easter week. Nothing else nearby seemed open or indicated signs of life.

A police car was parked outside my old house, though. Hopefully the officers were not investigating historic crimes dating back about, say, thirty years.

The family history dimension to Inverkeithing ticked off, I went on to investigate a bit more of the town.

Despite being a run-down place, there was a surprising number of medieval buildings clustered around the attractive Town House. Various other historic structures were dotted around the main street, including the quietly imposing St Peter's Kirk which although mainly Victorian featured a fourteenth century tower. Inverkeithing had clearly been a town of note once upon a time, though was now struggling in these post-industrial days. Its twentieth century era of ship breaking at the yard on the town's harbour was no more.

I passed a building with a plaque on it saying that the famous explorer David Livingstone had lived at the address "at various intervals between 1855 and 1865."

Why only "various intervals?" Did he keep getting evicted for rowdy behaviour? Did he have a tempestuous on-off relationship with his wife? Or was he forced to renounce his tenancy or ownership each time he headed off on his explorations to faraway lands?

The main street continued the town's theme of being a little faded. There were a few boarded up properties along it plus a couple of uninteresting looking pubs. There were various shops including a "Love Hurts tattoo parlour" (at least they were honest), a hair and beauty salon, and some charity shops. There was also a closed Chinese takeaway called Happy Palace. It looked neither happy nor palatial.

An interpretation board close to St Peter's Kirk told me something about the history of the town, the fact it was the birthplace of Samuel Greig, known as the father of the Russian navy, and some details about the Battle of Inverkeithing in 1651.

There was also, gloriously, a Gregg's bakery, allowing me to renew my acquaintance with their magnificent caramel fudge doughnuts, something I'd had to battle on bravely without since Kirkcaldy. As I sat eating my lunch of a couple of pies and the aforementioned doughnut on a park bench next to the church, I watched the quiet bustle of the street and enjoyed not having to walk anywhere. The pain and exhaustion in my legs was intensifying, but coming back to a past chapter of my life I felt a peaceful inner contentment.

Though that might just have been the caramel fudge doughnut.

Back at Inverkeithing station, I had plenty time until the next train. I went to the toilet in the station and I was taken aback by the gaunt reflection I saw in the mirror. I hadn't shaved since I left home, and I had bags under my eyes, making me look even more exhausted and worn out than I felt.

I was worried for a moment that I was ill, but I decided that the problem was that I had simply not realised how much walking I would do on my trip. Granted, I wasn't exactly exerting myself or breaking into much of a sweat. But even just the gentle, consistent ambling that I had been doing for five solid days now all surely added up to quite a workout. I calculated roughly that if I was spending two hours or more exploring each destination, then I was easily clocking up over ten miles' walking each day. Put like that, my adventure was a much more physically demanding endeavour than I had prepared myself for.

I needed to freshen up and have a proper rest, and I would be able to do that later on in the afternoon when I arrived at my day's final destination, South Queensferry. But I couldn't ease off yet – I had one more stop to take in. One last agonising push before the day was out.

CHAPTER 19: NORTH QUEENSFERRY

I arrived at the spectacular setting of North Queensferry station, the Forth Bridge now looming over me. North Queensferry as a village was a small place, and utterly dominated by a phenomenal feat of engineering. Opened in 1890, the Forth Bridge was the second-longest cantilever bridge in the world (and had been the longest until 1917 when the Quebec Bridge was built). Created to allow rail traffic between Edinburgh and the north of Scotland, it was both a vital lynchpin in the country's transport network and a world-famous icon of Scotland.

North Queensferry was a pleasant little village, with a dramatic setting on a peninsula of land right under the northern end of the bridge, the road bridge also visible just further along the firth. I began, though, by walking around the higher paths above the village on the way down from the station, which provided great views of the bridges and the hillsides around. The paths were rough and unattractively maintained, with gorse growing along the side, the occasional bench, and the odd abandoned little building – small brick structures that I guessed might be old wartime installations. Inside, one was curiously marked with the letters "FRC", which I assumed was "Forth Replacement Crossing". This was the (excuse the pun) forthcoming bridge that would replace the road bridge built in 1964 and already approaching its sell-by date. Perhaps the little hut was marked "FRC" as it was due for destruction in the building works. Either that or it was a hangout for workers on their lunch.

North Queensferry and my next stop across the water, South Queensferry, got their name from St Margaret, an eleventh century English princess who fled north after the Norman invasion of England and ended up marrying King Malcolm III of Scotland. Apparently she created a ferry link across the firth to enable pilgrimage from Edinburgh to Dunfermline Abbey. One of the names that had been mooted for the new road bridge was St Margaret's Crossing, though at the time of writing it has recently been announced that the name would be the rather unoriginal Queensferry Crossing.

A few boards were dotted around the village explaining not only the history of the area and the bridges but also the future bridge plans. Trains shot across the bridge every couple of minutes, streaks of Scotrail blue against the dark red paint of the bridge, a constant backdrop in sound as well as sight.

North Queensferry's biggest attraction – aside from the bridge, obviously – was Deep Sea World, a huge aquarium. It seemed busy from the crowds outside, and I had no interest in visiting, so I gave it a body swerve in favour of exploring the rest of the village itself. I walked through the narrow lanes, the bridge towering above like a skyscraper. I wandered along the small, rocky beach and around the core of the village. With the rail bridge on the left and the road bridge on the right, North Queensferry was a place both defined and bypassed by the bridges. I wondered how many people would visit, apart from to see Deep Sea World.

I walked under the bridge itself, which was, needless to say, an utter leviathan up close, and it induced not a little vertigo as I looked at the criss-crossed beams running between the main girders. It was a truly astonishing and awe-inspiring piece of engineering.

Nearby were the remains of the chapel of St James, with an inscription in one wall reading "this is done by the sailers of North Ferrie 1752". It was almost eerie to see the generations of history now dominated by the bridge – the Victorians clearly putting a massive stamp on everything else, almost like a full stop to history. The old walls, old gravestones, even the modern 1970s housing, all had the bridge lording over them, showing them who was master of this domain.

Down at the pier itself, there was a small lighthouse, built in 1817 by Robert Stevenson, grandfather of writer Robert Louis Stevenson and one of the famous "lighthouse Stevensons". There were a couple of folk with cameras, but little else of note. There was no big deal made of the bridges: just a few signs, and the pier standing quiet, an emerited testament to the success of the bridge.

Of course, the bridge didn't need anything or anyone to speak for it. Its presence was impossible to ignore. But a bit of celebration of this world-famous engineering marvel would not have gone amiss.

It contrasted very sharply with a bridge I saw later that year in France. Along with a group of friends, Nicole and I had a really enjoyable holiday road-tripping through the south of France. One of our highlights was the town of Millau, home to the highest bridge in the world, the Millau Viaduct, built in 2005. It boasted a fantastic museum that told the story of the bridge's creation and pioneering engineering, and there was a real sense of pride in this modern icon. While the Forth Bridge (if not the road bridge) was clearly a more impressive structure than the Millau Viaduct, the French structure certainly led the way in terms of celebrating its achievement.

I was delighted to hear some months after my rail journey, therefore, that the construction of the new Queensferry Crossing had sparked plans for some sort of visitor centre for what would now be the three Forth bridges.

It being mid-afternoon, I decided it was time for a pint, so I entered the Albert Hotel. I had seen it often enough while going past on the train, a large building with its name written on the side in white lettering. Years of advertising had finally paid off.

For a pub with one of the most iconic views in the country, it was a bit shabby on first impression. The range of drinks was basic, and there was just a handful of locals, plus a family on the other side of the pub that looked like tourists, and some rather minimalist furnishings including a few small bits of nautical paraphernalia on the walls. Mind you, the tourist and local groups both had children among them, and it's a reassuring indicator of a pub's atmosphere if there are children. The woman behind the bar was pleasant, and I paid £2.90 for a good pint of Best, which was the cheapest I could remember paying for a pint for a long time. The local crowd all seemed to know each other and were chatting and laughing away.

Suddenly, there was a power cut – the horseracing on TV went off, as did the lights, though oddly the slot machine was still flashing and the fridges still whirring. Nobody seemed concerned, and there were a few jokes about putting fifty pence in the meter. For some reason everything came back on again a few minutes later.

I sat contentedly at a table, resting my feet and writing up notes. I was increasingly exhausted and sore, and was glad to be close to the end of the day's travelling.

On my way out, a middle-aged couple approached me.

"You look like a local," said the man in a south of England accent.

"No, just a very good impression I'm afraid."

They were looking for directions to a post box. I didn't know where one was, so I referred them inside the pub for help, but as I walked on I turned back and noticed he didn't take up my suggestion. Perhaps he thought the pub was a bit rough. I should have stopped to reassure him.

Heading back up the steep hill to the railway station was a real struggle, my legs complaining at each step, and I was glad to be able to sit down at the station while I waited for my train. Across the tracks on the opposite platform was a huge mural portraying the rail bridge, ships, sea life and other aspects of North Queensferry. Fittingly, the bridge dominated the scene.

CHAPTER 20: DALMENY

It was a curious little journey, crossing the forth and then getting off straight away at the other side of the bridge. For what was something pretty momentous – crossing one of the world's most famous bridges – it was a journey of barely a couple of minutes on a regular commuter train. I wondered if anyone else ever did it just between those two stops.

I found myself paying much more attention to the views in those brief minutes than I normally would: the red roofs of houses, the large Deep Sea World car park, and smaller islands in the firth with their abandoned Second World War military installations that almost blended into the shape of the rock and were now covered in birds. It was tantalising to get a clear look for those few precious seconds before the beams of the first of the bridge's humps rushed past and turned the view to a blur.

I was so relieved to be nearly at my destination for the night, South Queensferry. However, I still had quite a walk ahead of me, and it was raining. The station was called Dalmeny, though subtitled "for South Queensferry" – perhaps they thought it would have been too confusing to have both Queensferries in the names of adjacent stations. In any case, the station wasn't really in either place, but in between – Dalmeny one side, South Queensferry (or, apparently, just

Queensferry, as it was correctly called) on the other. I could have stayed in either place, though I opted for South Queensferry because it was marginally closer, seemed to have more accommodation options, and was more visible from the train line and therefore held more curiosity for me.

It was a good fifteen minutes' walk through not particularly interesting parts of the town, mostly modern low-density sprawl, but thankfully all downhill. I soon arrived at the historic High Street. It had a grand, dark feel to it, Georgian and Victorian grandeur that suggested an Edinburgh in miniature.

After two nights of staying with friends, the lack of any contacts in the area meant I had resorted to booking a room in a hotel I found online. It was a very good price, and I discovered why when I found it was a non-en suite room in what was really more of a nightclub with rooms above it. My room, though small, was comfy and had a view of the road bridge. I was so happy to drop my bag off my shoulders, sit on the bed and know that this was my base until the next morning.

For a few moments I just sat, thankful for the opportunity to rest my legs. Then I noticed what looked like a bottle of vinegar on the bedside table. It was a small, square-based glass bottle with a little stopper that rested in the long, narrow neck, just like the wee decanters you might get on a table in a pub or restaurant next to the salt and pepper. It was filled with a brown liquid that looked exactly like vinegar.

Vinegar? In a hotel room? I thought for a moment. My first instinct was that it was to go with food, but then there was no salt alongside it. My next thought was that it was sherry or whisky, but that was an unusual thing to have as a complementary item in a fairly down-at-heel hotel room. Plus, it was a very generous serving, especially if it was whisky.

Gingerly, I picked it up, lifted off the lid, and had a smell. It smelt like sherry. Mind you, I'd heard of sherry vinegar, so was reluctant to have a swig. Noticing a small glass on the counter on the other side of the room, I went and got it and poured myself a small measure. I had a tiny taste.

Phew.

Sherry. Not vinegar. I poured myself a huge measure. Just the reward I needed after my long day of walking.

I decided to have a rest before I headed out to explore South Queensferry. I went over to the window and closed the blinds before lying down on the bed, sherry glass in hand. Much as I was walking a lot on my journey, I was concerned as to why I suddenly felt so mentally exhausted as well as just physically. My journey was gentle, even a bit dull in places. The weather was not oppressively hot. I wasn't emotionally drained by the stress of a strange culture, a language barrier, or an incomprehensible transport system. I was in Scotland. Barely three hours from home. That I couldn't put my finger on what was wrong with me merely unsettled me more, until I decided it was probably nothing more complicated than complete and utter exhaustion.

Musing over my thoughts, generous mouthfuls of sherry helped me relax and I soon fell asleep. I woke an hour later feeling a bit better, and then considerably more so after a shave, shower and change of clothes.

As evening approached, I headed out for food. I walked down the street and caught glimpses down side streets of the firth. The sky was a dark blue, the sunset lighting up the bridge into a seductive, glowing red that reflected on the still water. People were out and about. Laughter emanated from pubs. The town was livening up for a Friday night.

Given this was the last night of my trip I felt like I ought to treat myself. I had seen a curry house when first arriving in the town centre, and decided that would be a good place for my rather sad, solitary celebration. It was small and pokey, but the service was swift and excellent, and my chicken dhansak was wonderful.

Thankfully I didn't feel too self-conscious eating by myself among lots of other groups and couples, even without a charged phone on which to browse the web or Twitter. I had brought my notebook to catch up with my thoughts, and jotted down times and tickets for the next day from my timetable.

I also reviewed the costs I'd incurred on the journey so far. I'd bought tickets for some legs in advance with my vouchers, and for the others I'd only encountered a conductor on about half of them, saving me a few pounds here and there. Even including accommodation costs, my arithmetical jottings suggested my whole trip was sizing up to cost not much more than a couple of hundred pounds. Not bad for a six-day adventure across Scotland.

After eating, I wandered further into town to explore the High Street and search for a pub. It was now nearly dark, and South Queensferry was buzzing with small-town weekend atmosphere – including quite a few obvious tourists, cameras in hand.

An interpretation board on the street told me a few nuggets about the village and its history. The bridge, naturally, featured heavily. I learned, too, that the 1959 thriller film The 39 Steps was filmed in South Queensferry. And it reminded me that the village was also home to the Burryman Parade. In this bizarre local ritual, a man marches through the village covered head to toe in burrs, the sticky heads of burdock plants that grow around the local area. The origins of the centuries-old ritual appear to be lost in time, but there are probably few complaints from each Burryman, who is led through the town and fed whisky through a straw from various hostelries along the route. We can't even blame the peculiar custom on the long winter nights, as the parade is held in August of each year.

Along the length of the High Street ran lots of little lanes leading towards the water, down each of which the Forth Bridge could be seen. It was like the Paris cliché that the Eiffel Tower can be seen in the background of any street scene in the French capital; only here it was much more likely to be true given the size of the bridge and the High Street's journey parallel to the water front.

I passed several pubs, many of which seemed a bit noisy for the quiet mood I was in, and so I found one wee place at the end of the street that had the odd combination of friendly service, nice beer, pleasant decor, a few rough old men at the bar, and a music channel called "Vintage TV" on the screen. Its offering of bands like the Stone Roses and Kraftwerk were rather out of place with the pub's atmosphere and clientele, but right up my street.

After ordering a pint, I picked up a newspaper from a table and sat in the corner to read. It was the Daily Record, one of the less trashy and morally contemptible tabloids in Scotland, and I read it slowly, savouring my drink and enjoying just relaxing.

I suddenly became aware that one of the men at the bar seemed to be referring to me. I looked up.

"You're absolutely glued to that paper."

I wouldn't have minded if his tone was a cheeky attempt to engage me in banter, but it was unmistakeably into the realm of aggression. Perhaps I was easily irritable after five days on the road, but I decided to stand up to him, figuratively at least. I looked straight back at him.

"And is that problem for you?" I asked firmly but politely.

"No," he said, getting suddenly defensive. "I'm just saying you're absolutely glued to..."

"Well spotted," I interrupted sarcastically. I'm always up for a good-humoured chat with a stranger, but this wasn't good-humoured and I wanted him to be clear that I thought so. He was obviously just drunk and mouthing off, and maybe he didn't like seeing new people in his local pub.

Before he could say anything else, the barmaid, a feisty-looking middle-aged woman, intervened.

"Leave my customers alone," she chastised him. "Better reading the paper than listening to your boring chat."

That, thankfully, shut him up. It proved, though, as if there was any doubt, that such folk are tolerated in pubs like that purely because they put money behind the bar and not because the staff enjoy their company.

After finishing my pint I moved on to another place that seemed a little livelier. It was a bigger place, crowded inside, and there was football on the big screens. I worked my way through to the bar and was lucky to find a free stool. I perched on it, ordered a pint and in the absence of anything else to do I started watching the football.

I felt a little alone in this busy place. My phone was dead, everyone else around me was deep in animated conversation and celebrating the start of the weekend, and I had nothing to do but sip my pint. Time ticked by slowly, though the football – an English league match – presented a moderate distraction.

After finishing up, I decided to go to bed. It was after nine o'clock and now dark. The bridge looked stunning, lit up against the black sky and sea, and on my way back I saw the village's small harbour, a cluster of small boats gathered along the shoreline.

On my way back to the hotel I passed an immaculately dressed doorman outside what was clearly South Queensferry's token trendy wine bar. I could see through the bar and to the large windows at the back through which there were fine views of the bridge. The doorman was talking to two guys in jeans smoking. I couldn't quite hear what he was saying to them, but I think it was something about them not being smart enough to get in. The bar looked expensive, but people were no doubt paying for the view as much as the drinks.

Back at the hotel, there was a crowd outside and staff on the door. The nightclub was in full swing and was clearly bigger and noisier than I had first thought. I had neither desire, energy nor attire to join in. I headed up to bed, though not, for some considerable time, to sleep.

I left in the morning after a very nice breakfast in a cramped little dining room where I sat alone. I wondered if I had been the only guest in the hotel that night. The décor, like the rest of the hotel, was classic tartan kitsch – paintings of windswept, craggy moorlands and plates on the wall with prints of pipers in full Highland dress. A clock ticked loudly over the tinny little radio that played a local station's breakfast show.

I was relieved that it was the last day of my journey, as I

was still a bit weary, both from my full day yesterday and my broken night's sleep thanks to the nightclub. The end was in sight and I could properly relax soon. I had only three stops to go – South Gyle, Haymarket and Edinburgh Waverley itself. The walk back up the hill to Dalmeny station was gruelling. I hoped my energy would last out to the finishing line.

CHAPTER 21: SOUTH GYLE

South Gyle was a blink and you miss it sort of station, the Inverness train rushing through it and never stopping. On the outskirts of Edinburgh, it was a commuter stop, handy for some offices and major retail units, so the landscape around was all modern, bland and boxy. It was easy to not notice. I of course had to alight and explore it – it was all part of the journey even if I knew there was not much here of note.

The one thing I could guess about South Gyle was that it would be near the Gyle Centre, one of Edinburgh's huge out of town shopping complexes. My assumption that it was just a short walk was proved right by the map at the station, and I soon arrived there after a walk along a couple of streets of detached suburban houses and a busy dual carriageway lined with anonymous office complexes.

Walking through its car park, busy with Saturday morning shoppers off to spend their days in materialistic worship, the Gyle Centre was as big, bland and ugly as you can imagine shopping centres to be, but it would be a place to kill a bit of time. My first stop, after finding a toilet, was to call Nicole to keep her posted about my plans for the day. With my phone out of action, this required a phone box, something I don't think I had used for some years. I had to ask where one was from the information point, and was directed to an obscure, seemingly forgotten corner upstairs, far away from any shops. There were two phones, one broken. I wonder how often they were used, let alone maintained. Nicole's phone went to voicemail, and sixty pence had gone before I had the chance to finish my message. The only other coin I had was a pound, so after a total of one pound and sixty pence I'd finally completed my message. I remember the days when twenty pence was enough.

There was a Costa Coffee back downstairs near one of the entrances, and given I was still pretty weary I went to have a drink, a sit down and chill out. Finding a seat, I found myself feeling a little unwell again. Faint, too, but again probably just exhausted. Had I run myself into the ground just from walking about places? I found that hard to believe. I walked lots back home, including up mountains. Six days' walking in a row, though, was a scale of effort I'd not undertaken before.

It hardly helped that I was in this dreadful, bland place in the middle of nowhere. Everywhere around was noise, people with purpose, things to do, things to say. In the midst of it, me: sitting alone, weary, and starting to ask myself what the heck I was doing on an adventure that compelled me to spend time at the Gyle Centre.

South Gyle ended up being one of the few stops where I didn't quite exceed my two-hour minimum rule. Not that I cared.

CHAPTER 22: HAYMARKET

Haymarket was the station serving Edinburgh's west end, and the trains from Inverness to Edinburgh would always stop there as their penultimate stop. As the doors opened at Haymarket, the wheaty, full-bodied smell of the nearby Caledonian Brewery was absolutely heavenly. It was an evocative gateway to Edinburgh.

It was a strange station, in a way. Although big and busy, it was a relatively small space and existed only as a through station, trains rushing by every couple of minutes either west and northwards in one direction, or eastwards to Edinburgh's main station, Waverley – and often beyond, along the East Coast mainline to Newcastle and onwards to London. The two stations were at either end of a tunnel that took a few minutes to get through, a major piece of engineering that took the line underneath much of Edinburgh city centre.

The only other thing of note to me at Haymarket was Murrayfield stadium, Scotland's national rugby stadium, which the train passed right beside. I figured that because this was so iconic and so noticeable from the line I should go see it.

I'd been to Murrayfield once before, back in 1999. I was in Edinburgh with a group of friends from university and someone had got tickets to the rugby. It was Scotland v Spain in a World Cup match and it was stupifyingly boring, with a paltry crowd and a spectacular lack of atmosphere. Scotland won 49-0 and it was one of the least interesting sporting fixtures I've been to.

I walked out of Haymarket station and into the construction chaos of the tram works. The Edinburgh tram project had been one of the greatest scandals in recent years in Scotland. Trams had been removed in the 1950s (an arguably greater scandal) and there were plans to reintroduce lines to the city serving, among other places, the city centre, the airport and Leith.

Work began in 2008 but was delayed by technical problems, and then the contractor soon fell out with the arms-length company set up by the council to supervise things. Work ground to a halt as matters were referred to the courts. It took a long time for things to be sorted out and work finally restarted with an anticipated completion date of 2014, albeit vastly over-budget and with a much-shortened line. While I didn't agree with the argument that the trams should never have been built, I did accept that there were other Scottish cities with poorer public transport that could have benefitted more; and the scandal, delay and mounting cost was a disgusting waste, a shame on the city's administration and an embarrassment to its people.

For now, though, the city centre was a building site and the road outside Haymarket was a mess, with road works, diverted buses and terrible traffic jams. Posters in shop windows registered their discontent, and a unit that was a now-closed Ceramic Tile Warehouse had been plastered with messages such as "Coming soon... eventually... maybe... from a deserted street near you – Tramspotting" or "Did your councillor support the tram fiasco? Then vote them out!" There were plenty stories in the news about the effect on businesses all across the city centre, not least during the tourist seasons.

I walked away from all the roadworks and down towards to

the stadium. En route I passed Donaldson's College, the former home of Edinburgh's deaf school, another landmark you could see from the train. The building was for sale, according to a large sign, with detailed planning permission for apartments, the school seemingly having moved to new premises a few years back. It was a shame, as it was a stunning building with huge grounds. Built in 1851 in a breath-taking Gothic style, it looked like something from a fantasy novel, with brown stone in the typical Edinburgh style, tall towers at the corner, and ornate masonry. It was a shame it could not be bought for some civic purpose that could draw in the public to this architectural gem. Though with the trams, the people of Edinburgh probably had other more important planning decisions to be angry about.

The stadium was a lot further back in the opposite direction than it felt on the train. Like all big sports stadiums, even the oldest ones, it stuck out like a sore thumb against the surrounding rows of tenements and light industrial units. Sports stadiums always strike me as like spaceships that have landed in residential areas and have no hope of being unnoticed. They're not necessarily beautiful things, nor even ugly especially, just hideously out of place.

When I got to the gates around the stadium, I couldn't be bothered going through them. My body suddenly gave up on me, my legs screaming in protest. Every step, which I would have to retrace, seemed an enormous effort. I decided not to proceed. After all, it was just a stadium. And I didn't even like rugby.

CHAPTER 23: EDINBURGH WAVERLEY

It was a strange anticlimax getting off at Edinburgh Waverley. I'd done it. I'd finished. I'd gone stop by stop from Inverness to Edinburgh, all twenty-three stations in total, over the course of six days.

I was exhausted, and considerably more relieved than elated.

Amidst the noise and bustle of the busy station on a Saturday afternoon, not least with a crowd forming a peaceful protest in support of Palestine and the disruption of Waverley's massive ongoing refurbishment, I felt a little unsettled. The intense, echoey noise was strange and unfamiliar after more than five days in so many smaller places. Nobody noticed my presence. Nobody knew what I'd just done.

I knew Edinburgh well, of course, particularly the areas around where I worked and tended to stay, and near various friends I knew in the city. But I wasn't just going straight home. I still had to spend some time here exploring. I still, after all, had to subject Edinburgh to the same test as other places I'd visited: looking through fresh eyes, what did I think of it? How would I like it if I'd never been? Would I want to return?

I had one particular destination in mind to help me explore

these questions and gather my thoughts from the past week: the National Museum of Scotland. It was somewhere I'd never been in all my visits to Edinburgh, but I'd heard that there was a temporary exhibition of railway posters and art, and I thought this would be a fitting thing to do in my couple of hours.

Fighting my way through the crowds, out of the station and along the North Bridge, I took in the commanding views of Princes Street, the gardens, the Old Town, Waverley station beneath, and eastwards to Holyrood and Arthur's Seat. It was almost disconcerting to be on busy roads and among crowds after so many deathly quiet stops in the past week. After about five or ten minutes' walk I made it to the museum.

The exhibition was all about the portrayal and advertising of rail travel over the years, from the very early days where posters boasted about beating horse-drawn coaches, to the modern era, via the supposed golden age of the late Victorian era. There were a huge number of paintings, including many by the famous post-war railway painter Terence Cuneo, who incredibly climbed to the top of the Forth and Tay bridges to paint dramatic scenes of the railway lines. There was a video about different films that had been inspired by the railways, such as Brief Encounter and the Titfield Thunderbolt. Poetry, too, got a look in, as did many lovely posters and models from throughout the decades.

I wanted to try to get a sense from the exhibition about whether my trip was in the spirit of these attempts to capture a supposed golden age of travel. The exhibition, for me, evoked a sense of three things: discovery, adventure and romance.

I'd managed discovery, certainly. I'd explored many places I'd never been to, been pleasantly surprised by the most unlikely towns and villages, and seen some great scenery. From lesser-known charms like Newtonmore to surprises like Markinch and Kinghorn or the old chapel at Dalgety Bay, I'd stumbled across some wonderful nooks and crannies. And in the form of Ladybank or South Gyle, I'd discovered some dreadful ones too.

And it was often these surprising places that I ended up liking more than the more renowned tourist resorts such as Aviemore and Pitlochry. While it's easy to be impressed by places known for their beauty, it was in the more ordinary, out of the way towns and villages on the line where my expectations were low that I ended up being quite taken by. Those were the places where life was ticking along nicely, and where I wouldn't have expected anything extraordinary: but where a glimpse of serenity, beauty or quiet charm stood out as all the more special.

Secondly, adventure. Had I proved it was possible to have an adventure on the Scottish rail network? Well, although there had been little in the way of thrill, risk or adrenalin-fuelled excitement, I'd certainly travelled long distances, walked dozens of miles, and explored some lovely parts of Scotland. Moreover, my particular journey had never been done, to the best of my knowledge, by anyone else. Frankly, I'm not sure anyone would be so stupid. To the extent that I had been a pioneer – albeit at a gentle pace – I think it counted as an adventure.

And finally, as for romance, well, my wife will be delighted to read that there was nothing to report on that front from the past week's travel.

As for the other important question: would I return to Edinburgh? Of course I would. It was a beautiful city I could barely hope to scratch the surface of in a day, let alone two hours. It was brimming with history, exuding charm and inspiration from its centuries-old streets, and boasted a fine National Museum to which I knew I should return one day to see more of. It was a novelty being in Edinburgh for something other than work. If I hadn't been so shattered after my long trip, I would have enjoyed the exhilaration of having time on my hands to just explore Edinburgh at whim, without much in the way of responsibility or deadline.

One final thing I needed to ask myself: would I pay a bit more attention to the views out of the window on my journeys to and from Edinburgh, now I knew a little more about the places I passed through? I certainly hoped so. They'd no longer be mere names to half-hear in announcements, blurred images to barely notice out of the window. Each stop would be a place that would evoke memories, a place about which I could say "I've been there."

I walked back from the museum, and fittingly saw a Gregg's bakery across the road. One last caramel fudge doughnut was the least I deserved for a final, solitary moment of triumph.

Back at Waverley station, I scoured the departures board. Having taken six days to get here, it would be a much shorter journey home again.